ROWAN Junior

**Over thirty five knitting designs for
babies and children up to twelve years old**

Kim Hargreaves

ROWAN

Copyright © Rowan Yarns 2002
First published in Great Britain in 2002 by
Rowan Yarns Ltd
Green Lane Mill
Holmfirth
West Yorkshire
England
HD9 2DX

Internet: www.knitrowan.com
Email: rowanjunior@knitrowan.com

Designs & Styling Kim Hargreaves
Photographer Joey Toller
Hair & Make-up Annabel Hobbs
Models Perrin, Bryher, James, Fergus, Olivia, Cara, Harley, George,
Luca, Melissa, Ava, Grace, Zak, Alex, Josiah, Taylor, Olivia.
Book Design Kim Hargreaves
Design Co-ordinator Kathleen Hargreaves
Design Layout Les Dunford
Knitting co-ordinators Elizabeth Armitage & Lyndsay Kaye
Pattern writers Stella Smith & Sue Whiting

British Library Cataloguing in Publication Data
Rowan Yarns
Rowan Junior
1. Knitting - patterns
1 Title
ISBN 0-9540949-5-6

Printed by KHL Printing Co Pte Ltd
Singapore

Contents

*Lottie in 4ply Soft,
pattern page 58*

*Opposite Jasmine,
pattern page 74, this page
Evie, pattern page 51,
both in 4ply Cotton*

*Opposite Jo in Denim,
pattern page 62, this page
Felix in Handknit DK,
pattern page 79*

This page Rose in Wool Cotton, pattern page 64, opposite Lotus in Wool Cotton & All Seasons Cotton, pattern page 78

This page Jack, in Handknit DK, pattern page 54, opposite Jake in All Seasons Cotton, pattern page 65

Opposite Toby in Wool Cotton,
pattern page 56, this page
Grace in Rowanspun DK,
pattern page 71

*This page Luka in
Wool Cotton, pattern
page 48, opposite
Drew in Denim,
pattern page 52*

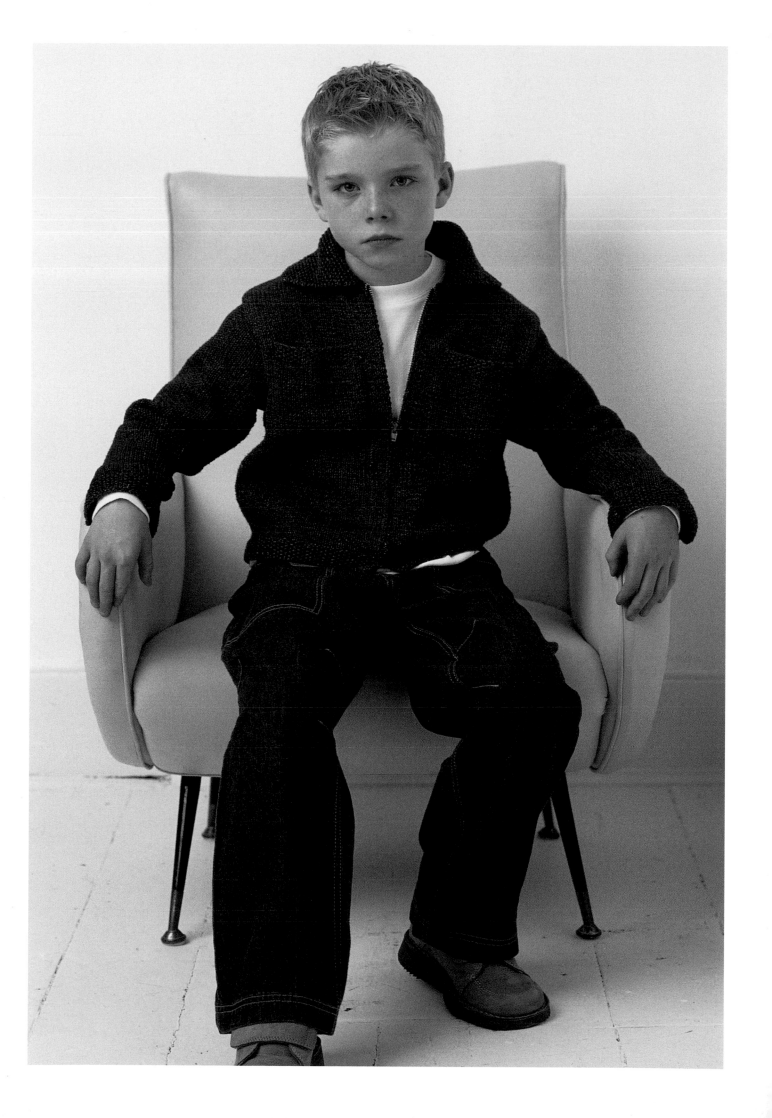

*This page Faye in
Wool Cotton &
All Seasons Cotton,
pattern page 57,
opposite Max in
All Seasons Cotton,
pattern page 47*

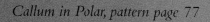
Callum in Polar, pattern page 77

Opposite Trixi in Wool Cotton, pattern page 68, this page Freddie in 4ply Soft, pattern page 61

Opposite Will, pattern page 59, this page Luka, pattern page 48 both in Wool Cotton

*Opposite Lou in Big Wool,
pattern page 67, this page
Grace in Rowanspun DK,
pattern page 71*

Opposite Mya in 4ply Soft,
pattern page 80,
this page Ellie in Polar,
pattern page 66

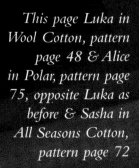

This page Luka in Wool Cotton, pattern page 48 & Alice in Polar, pattern page 75, opposite Luka as before & Sasha in All Seasons Cotton, pattern page 72

This page Lucy in Big Wool, pattern page 81 & Hannah in Polar, pattern page 76, opposite Luka in Wool Cotton, pattern page 48

Eliza in Polar,
pattern page 50 &
Amber in All Seasons
Cotton, pattern page 73

Grace in Rowanspun DK,
pattern page 71 & Jessie in
Kid Classic, pattern page 63

*Opposite Isla in
Kid Classic, pattern
page 73, this page
Dylan in 4ply Soft,
pattern page 76*

This page Sid in Big Wool, pattern page 55, opposite Eliza, pattern page 50 & Twinkle, pattern page 69, both in Polar

This page Luka in
Wool Cotton, pattern
page 48 & Sasha in
All Seasons Cotton,
pattern page 72,
opposite Hamish in
Rowanspun DK,
pattern page 46

This page Hannah in Polar, pattern page 76, opposite Jade in Big Wool, pattern page 73

Opposite Elliot in
Rowanspun DK,
pattern page 60,
opposite Eliza, pattern
page 50 & Zoe, pattern
page 70, both in Polar

THE KNITTING PATTERNS

The designs in this book are all sized according to Kim's original design and are graded accordingly. All of the garments are photographed on the correct size child; to help you to decide which size to knit we have numbered the sizes throughout the magazine to help you translate garments with the correct fit onto your child. To make this easier, there is a size diagram included with each pattern which shows not only the finished garment length and width but will also enable you to calculate the crucial centre-back to cuff measurement needed to ensure a perfect fit.

DESIGN NUMBER 1

HAMISH

YARN

Rowan Rowanspun DK

	6th	7th	8th	9th	10th	size
To fit age	4-5	6-7	8-9	9-10	11-12	years
To fit chest	61	66	71	76	81	cm
	24	26	28	30	32	in
A Chilli 732	2	2	2	2	3	x 50gm
B Punch 731	1	2	2	2	2	x 50gm

NEEDLES

1 pair 3¼mm (no 10) (US 3) needles
1 pair 4mm (no 8) (US 6) needles

TENSION

21 sts and 29 rows to 10 cm measured over stocking stitch using 4mm (US 6) needles.

BACK

Cast on 63 (69: 75: 81: 87) sts using 3¼mm (US 3) needles and yarn A.
Row 1 (RS): P3, *K3, P3, rep from * to end.
Row 2: K3, *P3, K3, rep from * to end.
These 2 rows form rib.

Work in rib for a further 10 rows, inc 1 st at each end of last row and ending with a WS row. 65 (71: 77: 83: 89) sts.
Change to 4mm (US 6) needles.
Beg with a K row, cont in st st until back measures 20 (23: 26: 28: 30) cm, ending with a WS row.

Shape armholes

Cast off 4 sts at beg of next 2 rows.
57 (63: 69: 75: 81) sts.
Dec 1 st at each end of next 4 (4: 6: 6: 6) rows, then on foll 2 (3: 2: 3: 4) alt rows.
45 (49: 53: 57: 61) sts.
Cont straight until armhole measures 15 (16: 17: 18: 19) cm, ending with a WS row.

Shape shoulders and back neck

Cast off 4 (4: 4: 5: 5) sts at beg of next 2 rows.
37 (41: 45: 47: 51) sts.
Next row (RS): Cast off 4 (4: 4: 5: 5) sts, K until there are 7 (8: 9: 8: 9) sts on right needle and turn, leaving rem sts on a holder.
Work each side of neck separately.
Cast off 4 sts at beg of next row.
Cast off rem 3 (4: 5: 4: 5) sts.
With RS facing, rejoin yarn to rem sts, cast off centre 15 (17: 19: 21: 23) sts, K to end.
Complete to match first side, reversing shapings.

FRONT

Cast on 63 (69: 75: 81: 87) sts using 3¼mm (US 3) needles and yarn A.
Work in rib as given for back for 12 rows, inc 1 st at each end of last row and ending with a WS row. 65 (71: 77: 83: 89) sts.
Change to 4mm (US 6) needles.
Beg with a K row, cont in st st as folls:
Join in yarn B.
Using yarn B, work 4 rows.
Using yarn A, work 4 rows.
Break off yarn A and cont using yarn B only.
Cont as given for back until 12 rows less have been worked than on back to start of shoulder shaping, ending with a WS row.

Shape neck

Next row (RS): K17 (18: 19: 20: 21) and turn, leaving rem sts on a holder.
Work each side of neck separately.
Dec 1 st at neck edge of next 4 rows, then on foll 2 alt rows. 11 (12: 13: 14: 15) sts.
Work 3 rows, ending with a WS row.

Shape shoulder

Cast off 4 (4: 4: 5: 5) sts at beg of next and foll alt row.
Work 1 row.
Cast off rem 3 (4: 5: 4: 5) sts.
With RS facing, rejoin yarn to rem sts, cast off centre 11 (13: 15: 17: 19) sts, K to end.
Complete to match first side, reversing shapings.

MAKING UP

PRESS as described on the information page.
Join right shoulder seam using back stitch, or mattress st if preferred.

Neckband

With RS facing, using 3¼mm (US 10) needles and yarn B, pick up and knit 16 sts down left side of neck, 11 (14: 14: 17: 20) sts from front, 16 sts up right side of neck, then 23 (26: 26: 29: 32) sts from back. 66 (72: 72: 78: 84) sts.
Next row (WS): *K3, P3, rep from * to end.
Rep this row 4 times more.
Cast off in rib.

Armhole borders (both alike)

With RS facing, using 3¼mm (US 10) needles and yarn B, pick up and knit 69 (75: 81: 81: 87) sts evenly around armhole edge.
Work in rib as given for back for 4 rows.
Cast off in rib.
See information page for finishing instructions.

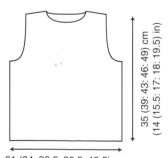

31 (34: 36.5: 39.5: 42.5) cm
(12 (13.5: 14.5: 15.5: 16.5) in)

35 (39: 43: 46: 49) cm
(14 (15.5: 17: 18: 19.5) in)

MAX

YARN

Rowan All Seasons Cotton

		1st	2nd	3rd	4th	5th	size
To fit age		months		years			
		0-6	6-12	1-2	2-3	3-4	
To fit chest		41	46	51	56	58	cm
		16	18	20	22	23	in
A Silver	173	1	2	2	2	2	x 50gm
B Valour	181	1	1	1	1	1	x 50gm
C Sooty	180	1	1	1	1	1	x 50gm
D Mellow	190	2	2	3	4	4	x 50gm

		6th	7th	8th	9th	10th	size
To fit age		4-5	6-7	8-9	9-10	11-12	years
To fit chest		61	66	71	76	81	cm
		24	26	28	30	32	in
A Silver	173	3	3	3	4	4	x 50gm
B Valour	181	1	1	1	1	1	x 50gm
C Sooty	180	1	1	1	1	1	x 50gm
D Mellow	190	5	6	6	7	8	x 50gm

NEEDLES

1 pair 4mm (no 8) (US 6) needles
1 pair 4½mm (no 7) (US 7) needles
1 pair 5mm (no 6) (US 8) needles

TENSION

17 sts and 24 rows to 10 cm measured over stocking stitch using 5mm (US 8) needles.

BACK

Cast on 43 (48: 53: 63: 68: 73: 78: 83: 93: 98) sts using 4½mm (US 7) needles and yarn A.
Row 1 (RS): K3, *P2, K3, rep from * to end.
Row 2: P3, *K2, P3, rep from * to end.
These 2 rows form rib.
Work in rib for a further 6 (6: 8: 8: 10: 10: 10: 12: 12: 12) rows, - (inc: inc: dec: dec: -: inc: inc: dec: dec) 1 st at - (one: both: both: one: -: one: both: both: one) end(s) of last row and ending with a WS row. 43 (49: 55: 61: 67: 73: 79: 85: 91: 97) sts.
Change to 5mm (US 8) needles.
Beg with a K row, cont in st st as folls:
Work 10 (12: 12: 14: 16: 17: 19: 23: 27: 29) rows, ending with a RS row.
Break off yarn A and join in yarn B.
Work 2 (2: 2: 2: 2: 3: 3: 3: 3: 3) rows.

Break off yarn B and join in yarn C.
Work 4 (4: 4: 4: 4: 6: 6: 6: 6: 6) rows, ending with a WS row.
Break off yarn C and join in yarn D.
Cont straight until back measures 12 (15: 17: 20: 23: 25: 28: 31: 33: 36) cm, ending with a WS row.
Shape armholes
Cast off 4 (4: 5: 5: 5: 6: 6: 7: 7: 7) sts at beg of next 2 rows.
35 (41: 45: 51: 57: 61: 67: 71: 77: 83) sts.
Cont straight until armhole measures 12 (13: 15: 16: 17: 19: 20: 21: 23: 24) cm, ending with a WS row.
Shape shoulders and back neck
Cast off 3 (4: 4: 5: 5: 6: 7: 7: 8: 8) sts at beg of next 2 rows. 29 (33: 37: 41: 47: 49: 53: 57: 61: 67) sts.
Next row (RS): Cast off 3 (4: 4: 5: 5: 6: 7: 7: 8: 8) sts, K until there are 6 (6: 7: 7: 10: 10: 10: 11: 11: 13) sts on right needle and turn, leaving rem sts on a holder.
Work each side of neck separately.
Cast off 3 (3: 3: 3: 4: 4: 4: 4: 4: 4) sts at beg of next row.
Cast off rem 3 (3: 4: 4: 6: 6: 6: 7: 7: 9) sts.
1st and 2nd sizes only
With RS facing, slip centre 11 (13: -: -: -: -: -: -: -: -) sts onto a holder, rejoin yarn to rem sts, K to end.
3rd, 4th, 5th, 6th, 7th, 8th, 9th and 10th sizes only
With RS facing, rejoin yarn to rem sts, cast off centre - (-: 15: 17: 17: 17: 19: 21: 23: 25) sts, K to end.
All sizes
Complete to match first side, reversing shapings.

FRONT

Work as given for back until 10 (10: 10: 12: 12: 12: 14: 14: 14: 14) rows less have been worked than on back to start of shoulder shaping, ending with a WS row.
Shape neck
Next row (RS): K14 (16: 17: 20: 22: 24: 27: 28: 30: 32) and turn, leaving rem sts on a holder.
Work each side of neck separately.
Dec 1 st at neck edge of next 4 rows, then on foll 1 (1: 1: 2: 2: 2: 3: 3: 3: 3) alt rows.
9 (11: 12: 14: 16: 18: 20: 21: 23: 25) sts.
Work 3 rows, ending with a WS row.
Shape shoulder
Cast off 3 (4: 4: 5: 5: 6: 7: 7: 8: 8) sts at beg of next and foll alt row.
Work 1 row.
Cast off rem 3 (3: 4: 4: 6: 6: 6: 7: 7: 9) sts.
1st and 2nd sizes only
With RS facing, slip centre 7 (9: -: -: -: -: -: -: -: -) sts onto a holder, rejoin yarn to rem sts, K to end.
3rd, 4th, 5th, 6th, 7th, 8th, 9th and 10th sizes only
With RS facing, rejoin yarn to rem sts, cast off centre - (-: 11: 11: 13: 13: 13: 15: 17: 19) sts, K to end.
All sizes
Complete to match first side, reversing shapings.

SLEEVES (both alike)

Cast on 28 (28: 33: 33: 33: 38: 38: 43: 43: 43) sts using 4½mm (US 7) needles and yarn A.
Work in rib as given for back for 8 (8: 10: 10: 12: 12: 12: 14: 14: 14) rows, dec (inc: dec: -: inc: dec: inc: dec: -: inc) 1 st at one (one: both: -: both: one: one: both: -: both) end(s) of last row and ending with a WS row.
27 (29: 31: 33: 35: 37: 39: 41: 43: 45) sts.

Change to 5mm (US 8) needles.
Beg with a K row and working first 8 (10: 10: 12: 12: 11: 13: 13: 15: 17) rows using yarn A, next 2 (2: 2: 2: 2: 3: 3: 3: 3: 3) rows using yarn B, foll 4 (4: 4: 4: 4: 6: 6: 6: 6: 6) rows using yarn C and then completing sleeve using yarn D, cont in st st as folls:
Inc 1 st at each end of 3rd and every foll alt row to 39 (35: 43: 43: 43: 49: 49: 45: 53: 51) sts, then on every foll 4th row until there are 41 (45: 51: 55: 57: 65: 69: 71: 79: 83) sts.
Cont straight until sleeve measures 15.5 (19.5: 21: 25: 26: 29.5: 34.5: 37: 40: 43) cm, ending with a WS row.
Cast off.

MAKING UP

PRESS as described on the information page.
Join right shoulder seam using back stitch, or mattress st if preferred.
Neckband
With RS facing, using 4mm (US 6) needles and yarn D, pick up and knit 14 (14: 15: 15: 15: 15: 17: 17: 17: 18) sts down left side of neck, 7 (10: 11: 11: 13: 13: 13: 15: 17: 19) sts from front, 14 (14: 15: 15: 15: 15: 17: 17: 17: 18) sts up right side of neck, then 18 (20: 22: 22: 25: 25: 26: 29: 32: 33) sts from back.
53 (58: 63: 63: 68: 68: 73: 78: 83: 88) sts.
Beg with a WS row, work in rib as given for back for 3 (3: 4: 5: 5: 5: 6: 6: 6: 6) cm.
Cast off **loosely** in rib.
See information page for finishing instructions, setting in sleeves using the square set-in method.

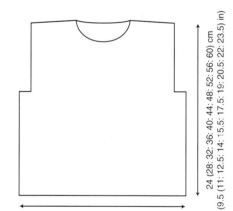

24 (28: 32: 36: 40: 44: 48: 52: 56: 60) cm
(9.5 (11: 12.5: 14: 15.5: 17.5: 19: 20.5: 22: 23.5) in)

25.5 (29: 32.5: 36: 39.5: 43: 46.5: 50: 53.5: 57) cm
(10 (11.5: 13: 14: 15.5: 17: 18.5: 19.5: 21: 22.5) in)

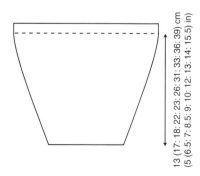

13 (17: 18: 22: 23: 26: 31: 33: 36: 39) cm
(5 (6.5: 7: 8.5: 9: 10: 12: 13: 14: 15.5) in)

LUKA

YARN

		1st	2nd	3rd	4th	5th	size
To fit age		months		years			
		0-6	6-12	1-2	2-3	3-4	
To fit chest		41	46	51	56	58	cm
		16	18	20	22	23	in

Rowan Wool Cotton

Plain sweater

A Camel	945	2	2	3	3	4	x 50gm
B Inky	908	2	2	2	2	2	x 50gm

Multi stripe sweater

A Gypsy	910	1	1	2	2	2	x 50gm
B Spark	947	1	1	1	1	1	x 50gm
C Rich	911	1	1	1	1	1	x 50gm
D Flower	943	1	1	1	1	1	x 50gm
E Tulip	944	1	1	1	1	1	x 50gm
F Citron	901	1	1	1	1	1	x 50gm
G Aqua	949	1	1	1	1	1	x 50gm
H Mango	950	1	1	1	1	1	x 50gm

Narrow stripe sweater

A Clear	941	2	3	3	3	4	x 50gm
B Inky	908	1	1	1	1	2	x 50gm

		6th	7th	8th	9th	10th	size
To fit age		4-5	6-7	8-9	9-10	11-12	years
To fit chest		61	66	71	76	81	cm
		24	26	28	30	32	in

Rowan Wool Cotton

Plain sweater

A Camel	945	4	4	5	5	6	x 50gm
B Inky	908	3	3	3	3	4	x 50gm

Multi stripe sweater

A Gypsy	910	2	2	2	3	3	x 50gm
B Spark	947	1	1	1	1	1	x 50gm
C Rich	911	1	2	2	2	2	x 50gm
D Flower	943	1	2	2	2	2	x 50gm
E Tulip	944	1	1	2	2	2	x 50gm
F Citron	901	1	1	1	1	1	x 50gm
G Aqua	949	1	1	1	1	1	x 50gm
H Mango	950	1	1	1	1	1	x 50gm

Narrow stripe sweater

A Clear	941	4	5	5	6	6	x 50gm
B Inky	908	2	2	2	2	3	x 50gm

NEEDLES

1 pair 3¼mm (no 10) (US 3) needles
1 pair 4mm (no 8) (US 6) needles

TENSION

22 sts and 30 rows to 10 cm measured over stocking stitch using 4mm (US 6) needles.

Plain sweater
BACK
Cast on 52 (57: 62: 67: 72: 77: 82: 87: 97: 102) sts using 3¼mm (US 3) needles and yarn B.
Row 1 (RS): P2,★ K3, P2, rep from ★ to end.
Row 2: K2, ★ P3, K2, rep from ★ to end.
These 2 rows form rib.
Work in rib for a further 6 rows, dec (-: inc: inc: inc: -: inc: inc: dec: dec) 1 st at one (-: one: both: one: -: one: both: both: one) end(s) of last row and ending with a WS row.
51 (57: 63: 69: 73: 77: 83: 89: 95: 101) sts.
Change to 4mm (US 6) needles.
Beg with a K row, cont in st st as folls:
Cont straight until back measures 17 (19: 21: 23: 25: 27: 28: 29: 30: 31) cm, ending with a WS row.
Shape raglan armholes
Cast off 2 (3: 3: 4: 4: 4: 5: 5: 5: 5) sts at beg of next 2 rows. 47 (51: 57: 61: 65: 69: 73: 79: 85: 91) sts.
Dec 1 st at each end of next 1 (1: 3: 5: 5: 7: 7: 11: 13: 17) rows, then on every foll alt row until 19 (21: 23: 23: 25: 25: 27: 27: 29: 29) sts rem, ending with a RS row.
Dec 0 (1: 1: 1: 1: 1: 1: 1: 1: 1) st at each end of next row, ending with a WS row.
1st and 2nd sizes only
Leave rem 19 sts on a holder.
3rd, 4th, 5th, 6th, 7th, 8th, 9th and 10th sizes
Cast off rem - (-: 21: 21: 23: 23: 25: 25: 27: 27) sts.

FRONT
Using yarn A, ★★ work as given for back until 31 (33: 35: 35: 37: 39: 41: 41: 45: 45) sts rem in raglan shaping.
Work 1 row, ending with a WS row.
Shape neck
Next row (RS): K2tog, K7 (7: 7: 7: 7: 10: 10: 10: 13: 13) and turn, leaving rem sts on a holder.
Work each side of neck separately.
Dec 1 st at neck edge of next 4 (4: 4: 4: 4: 6: 6: 8: 8) rows **and at same time** dec 1 st at raglan edge of 2nd and every foll alt row. 2 sts.
Work 1 row, ending with a WS row.

Next row (RS): K2tog and fasten off.
1st and 2nd sizes only
With RS facing, slip centre 13 (15: -: -: -: -: -: -: -: -) sts onto a holder, rejoin yarn to rem sts, K to last 2 sts, K2tog.
3rd, 4th, 5th, 6th, 7th, 8th, 9th and 10th sizes
With RS facing, rejoin yarn to rem sts, cast off centre - (-: 17: 17: 19: 15: 17: 17: 15: 15) sts, K to last 2 sts, K2tog.
All sizes
Complete to match first side, reversing shapings.

SLEEVES
Cast on 27 (27: 32: 32: 37: 37: 37: 42: 42: 47) sts using 3¼mm (US 3) needles and yarn B.
Work in rib as given for back for 8 rows, - (inc: dec: inc: dec: -: inc: dec: inc: dec) 1 st at - (both: one: one: both: -: both: one: one: both) end(s) of last row and ending with a WS row.
27 (29: 31: 33: 35: 37: 39: 41: 43: 45) sts.
Change to 4mm (US 6) needles.
Beg with a K row, working first 8 (8: 8: 10: 10: 10: 12: 12: 12: 12) rows using yarn B, foll 4 rows using yarn A, foll 6 rows using yarn B and then completing sleeve using yarn A, cont in st st as folls:
★★Inc 1 st at each end of next and every foll 4th (4th: 4th: 6th: 6th: 6th: 6th: 6th: 8th: 8th) row to 39 (47: 53: 39: 45: 49: 61: 71: 51: 63) sts, then on every foll alt (alt: alt: 4th: 4th: 4th: 4th: -: 6th: 6th) row until there are 47 (51: 55: 59: 63: 67: 69: -: 73: 75) sts.
Cont straight until sleeve measures 14 (17: 20: 23: 26: 29: 32: 35: 38: 41) cm, ending with a WS row.
Shape raglan
Cast off 2 (3: 3: 4: 4: 4: 5: 5: 5: 5) sts at beg of next 2 rows. 43 (45: 49: 51: 55: 59: 59: 61: 63: 65) sts.
Dec 1 st at each end of next 7 (7: 9: 7: 9: 11: 7: 7: 7: 7) rows, then on every foll alt row until 15 (15: 15: 17: 17: 17: 19: 19: 19: 19) sts rem.
Work 1 row, ending with a WS row.
Left sleeve only
Dec 1 st at each end of next row, then cast off 2 (2: 2: 3: 3: 3: 3: 3: 3: 3) sts at beg of foll row.
11 (11: 11: 12: 12: 12: 14: 14: 14: 14) sts.
Dec 1 st at beg of next row, then cast off 3 (3: 3: 3: 3: 3: 4: 4: 4: 4) sts at beg of foll row.
7 (7: 7: 8: 8: 8: 9: 9: 9: 9) sts.

Rep last 2 rows once more.
3 (3: 3: 4: 4: 4: 4: 4: 4) sts.
Right sleeve only
Cast off 3 (3: 3: 4: 4: 4: 4: 4: 4) sts at beg and dec 1 st at end of next row.
11 (11: 11: 12: 12: 12: 14: 14: 14) sts.
Work 1 row.
Cast off 3 (3: 3: 3: 3: 3: 3: 4: 4) sts at beg and dec 1 st at end of next row.
7 (7: 7: 8: 8: 8: 9: 9: 9) sts.
Work 1 row.
Rep last 2 rows once more.
3 (3: 3: 4: 4: 4: 4: 4: 4) sts.
Both sleeves
Cast off rem 3 (3: 3: 4: 4: 4: 4: 4: 4) sts.

Multi stripe sweater
STRIPE SEQUENCE
Beg with a K row, work in st st in colours as folls:
Rows 1 and 2: Using yarn A.
Rows 3 and 4: Using yarn C.
Row 5: Using yarn H.
Row 6: Using yarn B.
Row 7: Using yarn D.
Rows 8 and 9: Using yarn A.
Rows 10 and 11: Using yarn E.
Row 12: Using yarn G.
Rows 13 to 15: Using yarn C.
Rows 16 and 17: Using yarn H.
Row 18: Using yarn F.
Row 19: Using yarn B.
Row 20: Using yarn H.
Row 21: Using yarn A.
Rows 22 and 23: Using yarn C.
Rows 24 to 27: Using yarn D.
Rows 28 and 29: Using yarn A.
Row 30: Using yarn E.
Row 31: Using yarn F.
Rows 32 and 33: Using yarn G.
Rows 34 and 35: Using yarn E.
Row 36: Using yarn D.
Rows 37 and 38: Using yarn B.
Rows 39 to 41: Using yarn C.
Row 42: Using yarn A.
Row 43: Using yarn H.
Row 44: Using yarn F.
Rows 45 and 46: Using yarn E.
Rows 47 and 48: Using yarn A.
Row 49: Using yarn G.
Rows 50 and 51: Using yarn F.
Rows 52 and 53: Using yarn B.
Row 54: Using yarn H.
Rows 55 and 56: Using yarn D.
Rows 57 and 58: Using yarn A.
Rows 59 to 61: Using yarn C.
Row 62: Using yarn D.
Row 63: Using yarn B.
Row 64: Using yarn H.
Row 65: Using yarn A.
Row 66: Using yarn D.
Rows 67 and 68: Using yarn E.
Row 69: Using yarn A.
Rows 70 and 71: Using yarn G.

Row 72: Using yarn F.
Row 73: Using yarn A.
Row 74: Using yarn E.
Rows 75 and 76: Using yarn D.
Rows 77 to 79: Using yarn C.
Rows 80 and 81: Using yarn A.
Row 82: Using yarn G.
Row 83: Using yarn E.
Row 84: Using yarn E.
Rows 85 and 86: Using yarn D.
Rows 87 and 88: Using yarn C.
Rows 89 and 90: Using yarn B.
Row 91: Using yarn H.
Row 92: Using yarn F.
Rows 93 to 95: Using yarn G.
Rows 96 and 97: Using yarn D.
Row 98: Using yarn A.
Row 99: Using yarn E.
Row 100: Using yarn G.
Rows 101 to 103: Using yarn E.
Rows 104 and 105: Using yarn A.
Row 106: Using yarn H.
Row 107: Using yarn B.
Rows 108 to 110: Using yarn C.
Row 111: Using yarn D.
Row 112: Using yarn E.
Row 113: Using yarn A.
Row 114: Using yarn F.
Row 115: Using yarn H.
Row 116: Using yarn B.
Rows 117 and 118: Using yarn C.
Rows 119 to 121: Using yarn A.
Row 122: Using yarn D.
Rows 123 and 124: Using yarn E.
Row 125: Using yarn F.
Rows 126 and 127: Using yarn G.
Row 128: Using yarn E.
These 128 rows form stripe sequence and should be repeated if required.

1st, 2nd, 3rd, 4th and 5th sizes only
Work back, front and sleeves as given for plain sweater using colours as folls: Work rib on all pieces using yarn A, then work in stripe sequence (as detailed above), beg back and front with stripe row 1 (1: 1: 1: 3: -: -: -: -: -) and sleeves with stripe row 11 (7: 5: 1: 1: -: -: -: -: -). Raglan armhole shaping on all pieces should beg after stripe row 44 (50: 56: 62: 70: -: -: -: -: -).

6th, 7th, 8th, 9th and 10th sizes only
BACK
Cast on - (-: -: -: -: 77: 82: 87: 97: 102) sts using 3¼mm (US 3) needles and yarn A.
Row 1 (RS): P2,★ K3, P2, rep from ★ to end.
Row 2: K2, ★ P3, K2, rep from ★ to end.
These 2 rows form rib.
Work in rib for a further 6 rows, - (-: -: -: -: -: inc: inc: dec: dec) - (-: -: -: -: -: 1: 2: 2: 1) st(s) evenly across last row and ending with a WS row. - (-: -: -: -: 77: 83: 89: 95: 101) sts.

Change to 4mm (US 6) needles.
Beg with row - (-: -: -: -: 7: 13: 19: 25: 31), now work in stripe sequence (as detailed above) as folls:
Work - (-: -: -: -: 2: 2: 2: 2: 2) rows.
Dec 1 st at each end of next and every foll 6th row to - (-: -: -: -: 71: 77: 83: 89: 95) sts, then on every foll 4th row until - (-: -: -: -: 67: 73: 77: 83: 89) sts rem.
Work - (-: -: -: -: 7: 7: 7: 7: 9) rows, ending with a WS row.
Inc 1 st at each end of next and every foll 8th row to - (-: -: -: -: 77: 83: 87: 93: 99) sts, then on foll - (-: -: -: -: -: 6th: 6th: 6th) row until there are - (-: -: -: -: -: 89: 95: 101) sts.
Cont straight until back measures approx - (-: -: -: -: 27: 28: 29: 30: 31) cm, ending after stripe row - (-: -: -: -: 80: 88: 98: 106: 116) and with a WS row.
Complete as given for back of plain sweater from beg of raglan armhole shaping.

FRONT
Working side seam shaping and stripes as set by back, work as given for front of plain sweater from ★★.

SLEEVES
Work as given for plain sweater, working rib using yarn A, and then working in stripe sequence (as detailed above), beg with stripe row - (-: -: -: -: 1: 1: 1: 1: 1). Raglan shaping should beg after stripe row - (-: -: -: -: 80: 88: 98: 106: 116).

Narrow stripe sweater
STRIPE SEQUENCE
Beg with a K row, work in st st in colours as folls:
Rows 1 and 2: Using yarn A.
Rows 3 and 4: Using yarn B.
Rows 5 to 10: Using yarn A.
These 10 rows form stripe sequence.

1st, 2nd, 3rd, 4th and 5th sizes only
Work back, front and sleeves as given for plain sweater using colours as folls: Work rib on all pieces using yarn A, then work in stripe sequence (as detailed above), beg back and front with stripe row 1 (1: 1: 1: 1: -: -: -: -: -) and sleeves with stripe row 1 (7: 5: 1: 9: -: -: -: -: -). Raglan armhole shaping on all pieces should beg after stripe row 4 (10: 6: 2: 8: -: -: -: -: -).

6th, 7th, 8th, 9th and 10th sizes only
Work back, front and sleeves as given for multi stripe sweater using colours as folls: Work rib on all pieces using yarn A, then work in stripe sequence (as detailed above), beg back and front with stripe row - (-: -: -: -: 1: 1: 1: 1: 1) and sleeves with stripe row - (-: -: -: -: 5: 9: 3: 7: 1). Raglan armhole shaping on all pieces should beg after stripe row - (-: -: -: -: 4: 6: 10: 2: 6).

1st, 2nd, 3rd, 4th & 5th sizes

27 (30: 32: 35: 38) cm (10.5 (12: 12.5: 14: 15) in)

23 (26: 28.5: 31.5: 33) cm (9 (10: 11: 12.5: 13) in)

14 (17: 20: 23: 26) cm (5.5 (6.5: 8: 9: 10) in)

6th, 7th, 8th, 9th & 10th sizes

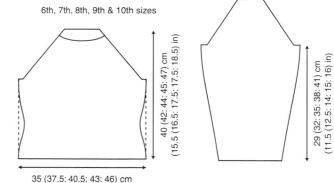

40 (42: 44: 45: 47) cm (15.5 (16.5: 17.5: 17.5: 18.5) in)

35 (37.5: 40.5: 43: 46) cm (14 (15: 16: 17: 18) in)

29 (32: 35: 38: 41) cm (11.5 (12.5: 14: 15: 16) in)

MAKING UP

PRESS as described on the information page. Join both front and right back raglan seams using back stitch, or mattress st if preferred.

Plain sweater

Neckband

With RS facing, using 3¼mm (US 3) needles and yarn B, pick up and knit 9 (11: 11: 11: 11: 12: 12: 13: 13) sts from left sleeve, 25 (27: 29: 29: 31: 31: 33: 33: 33) sts from front, 9 (10: 11: 11: 11: 11: 12: 12: 13: 13) sts from right sleeve, then 19 (19: 21: 21: 24: 24: 25: 25: 28: 28) sts from back.
62 (67: 72: 72: 77: 77: 82: 82: 87: 87) sts.
Beg with a WS row, work in rib as given for back for 6 rows.
Cast off **loosely** in rib.

Multi and narrow stripe sweaters

Neckband

With RS facing, using 3¼mm (US 3) needles and yarn A, pick up and knit 9 (11: 11: 11: 11: 12: 12: 13: 13) sts from left sleeve, 25 (27: 29: 29: 31: 31: 33: 33: 33) sts from front, 9 (10: 11: 11: 11: 11: 12: 12: 13: 13) sts from right sleeve, then 19 (19: 21: 21: 24: 24: 25: 25: 28: 28) sts from back. 62 (67: 72: 72: 77: 77: 82: 82: 87: 87) sts.
Beg with a K row, work in rev st st for 5 rows.
Cast off **loosely** purlwise.

All sweaters

See information page for finishing instructions.

DESIGN NUMBER 4

ELIZA

YARN

	6th	7th	8th	9th	10th	size
To fit age	4-5	6-7	8-9	9-10	11-12	years
To fit chest	61	66	71	76	81	cm
	24	26	28	30	32	in

Rowan Polar
        4   4   4   5   5 x100gm
(photographed in Winter White 645)

NEEDLES

1 pair 7mm (no 2) (US 10½) needles
1 pair 8mm (no 0) (US 11) needles

TENSION

12 sts and 16 rows to 10 cm measured over stocking stitch using 8mm (US 11) needles.

BACK

Cast on 41 (45: 47: 51: 53) sts using 7mm (US 10½) needles.
Row 1 (RS): P1, *K1, P1, rep from * to end.
Row 2: K1, *P1, K1, rep from * to end.
These 2 rows form rib.
Work in rib for a further 6 rows, ending with a WS row.
Change to 8mm (US 11) needles.
Next row (RS): K2, M1, K to last 2 sts, M1, K2.
Working all increases as set by last row and beg with a P row, cont in st st as folls:

Inc 1 st at each end of 4th (6th: 6th: 8th: 8th) and every foll 6th row until there are 49 (53: 55: 59: 61) sts.
Cont straight until back measures 19 (20: 21: 22: 23) cm, ending with a WS row.
Shape raglan armholes
Cast off 3 sts at beg of next 2 rows.
43 (47: 49: 53: 55) sts.
Next row (RS): P2, K2tog, K to last 4 sts, K2tog tbl, P2.
Next row: K2, P2tog tbl, P to last 4 sts, P2tog, K2.
Working all raglan decreases as set by last 2 rows, dec 1 st at each end of next 3 rows, then on every foll alt row until 15 (17: 17: 19: 19) sts rem.
Work 1 row, ending with a WS row.
Cast off rem 15 (17: 17: 19: 19) sts.

FRONT

Work as given for back until 25 (27: 27: 31: 31) sts rem in raglan shaping.
Work 1 row, ending with a WS row.
Shape neck
Next row (RS): P2, K2tog, K4 (4: 4: 6: 6) and turn, leaving rem sts on a holder.
Work each side of neck separately.
Dec 1 st at neck edge of next 3 rows and at same time dec 1 st at raglan edge on 2nd of these rows. 3 (3: 3: 5: 5) sts.
9th and 10th sizes only
Next row (RS): P2, K3tog. 3 sts.
Next row: P1, K2.
All sizes
Next row (RS): P3tog.
Next row: K1 and fasten off.
With RS facing, rejoin yarn to rem sts, cast off centre 9 (11: 11: 11: 11) sts, K to last 4 sts, K2tog tbl, P2.
Complete to match first side, reversing shapings.

SLEEVES

Cast on 25 (27: 29: 31: 33) sts using 7mm (US 10½) needles.
Work in rib as given for back for 12 rows, ending with a WS row.
Change to 8mm (US 11) needles.
Working all increases as set by back and beg with a K row, cont in st st, shaping sides by inc 1 st at each end of 3rd and every foll 8th (10th: 10th: 12th: 12th) row until there are 33 (35: 37: 39: 41) sts.
Cont straight until sleeve measures 30 (32: 34: 36: 38) cm, ending with a WS row.
Shape raglan
Cast off 3 sts at beg of next 2 rows.
27 (29: 31: 33: 35) sts.
Next row (RS): P2, K2tog, K to last 4 sts, K2tog tbl, P2.
Next row: K2, P to last 2 sts, K2.

Working all raglan decreases as set by last 2 rows, dec 1 st at each end of 3rd and every foll 4th row to 21 (23: 25: 27: 29) sts, then on every foll alt row until 11 sts rem.
Work 1 row, ending with a WS row.
Left sleeve only
Dec 1 st at each end of next row. 9 sts.
Cast off 2 sts at beg of next row. 7 sts.
Dec 1 st at beg of next row, then cast off 3 sts at beg of foll row. 3 sts.
Right sleeve only
Cast off 3 sts at beg and dec 1 st at end of next row. 7 sts.
Work 1 row. Rep last 2 rows once more. 3 sts.
Both sleeves
Cast off rem 3 sts.

MAKING UP

PRESS as described on the information page. Join both front and right back raglan seams using back stitch, or mattress st if preferred.

Neckband

With RS facing and using 7mm (US 10½) needles, pick up and knit 9 sts from left sleeve, 6 (6: 6: 8: 8) sts down left side of neck, 9 (11: 11: 11: 11) sts from front, 6 (6: 6: 8: 8) sts up right side of neck, 9 sts from right sleeve, then 14 (16: 16: 18: 18) sts from back. 53 (57: 57: 63: 63) sts.
Work in rib as given for back for 7 cm.
Cast off in rib.
See information page for finishing instructions.

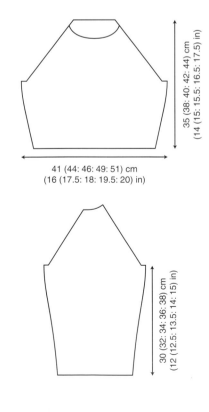

41 (44: 46: 49: 51) cm
(16 (17.5: 18: 19.5: 20) in)

35 (38: 40: 42: 44) cm
(14 (15: 15.5: 16.5: 17.5) in)

30 (32: 34: 36: 38) cm
(12 (12.5: 13.5: 14: 15) in)

EVIE

YARN

	1st	2nd	3rd	4th	5th	size
To fit age	months		years			
	0-6	6-12	1-2	2-3	3-4	
To fit chest	41	46	51	56	58	cm
	16	18	20	22	23	in
Rowan 4 ply Cotton						
		2	3	3	4	4 x 50gm

	6th	7th	8th	9th	10th	size
To fit age	4-5	6-7	8-9	9-10	11-12	years
To fit chest	61	66	71	76	81	cm
	24	26	28	30	32	in
Rowan 4 ply Cotton						
	5	6	7	8	9	x 50gm

(photographed in Lemongrass 122)
Oddment of same yarn in contrast colour
(Nightsky 115) for optional flower trim

NEEDLES

1 pair 2¼mm (no 13) (US 1) needles
1 pair 3mm (no 11) (US 2/3) needles

BUTTONS - 1 x 75333

TENSION

28 sts and 38 rows to 10 cm measured over
stocking stitch using 3mm (US 2/3) needles.

Pattern note: As row end edges of back
opening form actual finished edges of garment,
it is important these edges are kept neat.
Therefore all new balls of yarn should be joined
in at armhole edges of rows.

BACK

Cast on 69 (77: 85: 93: 101: 109: 117: 125: 133:
141) sts using 2¼mm (US 1) needles.
Row 1 (RS): K1, *P1, K1, rep from * to end.
Row 2: As row 1.
These 2 rows form moss st.
Work in moss st for a further 6 rows, ending
with a WS row.
Change to 3mm (US 2/3) needles.
Beg with a K row, cont in st st as folls:
Cont straight until back measures 12 (14: 16: 19:
22: 25: 28: 31: 34: 37) cm, ending with a WS row.

Shape armholes

Cast off 4 (4: 4: 4: 4: 5: 5: 5: 5: 5) sts at beg of
next 2 rows.
61 (69: 77: 85: 93: 99: 107: 115: 123: 131) sts.
Dec 1 st at each end of next 5 (5: 5: 5: 5: 6: 6: 6:
6: 6) rows.
51 (59: 67: 75: 83: 87: 95: 103: 111: 119) sts.
Cont straight until armhole measures 6 (8: 10: 11:
12: 13: 14: 15: 16: 17) cm, ending with a WS row.

Divide for back opening

Next row (RS): K25 (29: 33: 37: 41: 43: 47: 51:
55: 59) and turn, leaving rem sts on a holder.
Work each side of neck separately.
Cont straight until armhole measures 11 (13: 15:
16: 17: 18: 19: 20: 21: 22) cm, ending with a WS
row.

Shape shoulder and back neck

Cast off 4 (5: 7: 8: 9: 9: 10: 11: 12: 13) sts at beg
of next row, then 8 (9: 9: 10: 11: 12: 13: 14: 15:
16) sts at beg of foll row, ending with a WS row.
Cast off 4 (5: 7: 8: 9: 9: 10: 11: 12: 13) sts at beg
of next row, then 4 sts at beg of foll row, ending
with a WS row.
Cast off rem 5 (6: 6: 7: 8: 9: 10: 11: 12: 13) sts.
With RS facing, rejoin yarn to rem sts, K2tog,
K to end.
Complete to match first side, reversing shapings.

FRONT

Work as given for back until 14 (14: 14: 16: 16:
16: 18: 18: 18: 18) rows less have been worked
than on back to start of **shoulder** shaping,
ending with a WS row.

Shape neck

Next row (RS): K19 (22: 26: 30: 33: 34: 38: 41:
44: 47) and turn, leaving rem sts on a holder.
Work each side of neck separately.
Dec 1 st at neck edge of next 4 rows, then on
foll 1 (1: 1: 2: 2: 2: 3: 3: 3: 3) alt rows, then on foll
4th row. 13 (16: 20: 23: 26: 27: 30: 33: 36: 39) sts.
Work 3 rows, ending with a WS row.

Shape shoulder

Cast off 4 (5: 7: 8: 9: 9: 10: 11: 12: 13) sts at beg
of next and foll alt row.
Work 1 row.
Cast off rem 5 (6: 6: 7: 8: 9: 10: 11: 12: 13) sts.
With RS facing, rejoin yarn to rem sts, cast off
centre 13 (15: 15: 15: 17: 19: 19: 21: 23: 25) sts,
K to end.
Complete to match first side, reversing shapings.

SLEEVES (both alike)

Cast on 45 (47: 49: 51: 53: 55: 57: 59: 61: 63) sts
using 2¼mm (US 1) needles.
Work in moss st as for back for 8 rows, ending
with a WS row.
Change to 3mm (US 2/3) needles.
Beg with a K row, cont in st st, inc 1 st at each
end of next and every foll 6th (6th: 4th: 4th: 4th:
4th: 4th: 6th: 6th: 6th) row to 57 (51: 73: 85: 93:
99: 107: 69: 69: 75) sts, then on every foll 4th (4th:
alt: alt: alt: alt: –: 4th: 4th: 4th) row until there are
61 (73: 85: 89: 95: 101: –: 111: 117: 123) sts.
Cont straight until sleeve measures 15 (18: 21:
24: 27: 30: 33: 36: 39: 42) cm, ending with a WS
row.

Shape top

Cast off 4 (4: 4: 4: 4: 5: 5: 5: 5: 5) sts at beg of
next 2 rows.
53 (65: 77: 81: 87: 91: 97: 101: 107: 113) sts.
Dec 1 st at each end of next and foll 4 (4: 4: 4: 4:
5: 5: 5: 5: 5) rows.
Work 1 row, ending with a WS row.
Cast off rem 43 (55: 67: 71: 77: 79: 85: 89: 95:
101) sts.

MAKING UP

PRESS as described on the information page.
Join shoulder seams using back stitch, or mattress
st if preferred.

Neckband

With RS facing and using 2¼mm (US 1)
needles, starting and ending at top of back
opening, pick up and knit 12 (13: 13: 14: 15: 16:
17: 18: 19: 20) sts from left back neck, 18 (18: 18:
20: 20: 20: 22: 22: 22: 22) sts down left side of
neck, 13 (15: 15: 15: 17: 19: 19: 21: 23: 25) sts
from front, 18 (18: 18: 20: 20: 20: 22: 22: 22: 22)
sts up right side of neck, then 12 (13: 13: 14: 15:
16: 17: 18: 19: 20) sts from right back neck.
73 (77: 77: 83: 87: 91: 97: 101: 105: 109) sts.
Work in moss st as given for back for 4 rows.
Cast off in moss st.
See information page for finishing instructions,
setting in sleeves using the shallow set-in
method. Make button loop and attach button at
ends of neckband to fasten back neck.

Flower (optional)

Following instructions given for flower of Alice
bag and using 2¼mm (US 1) needles, make
flower using main colour yarn for petals and
oddment of contrast colour for centre. Attach
flower as in photograph.

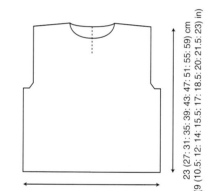

24.5 (27.5: 30.5: 33: 36: 39: 42: 44.5: 47.5: 50.5) cm
(9.5 (11: 12: 13: 14: 15.5: 16.5: 17.5: 18.5: 20) in)

23 (27: 31: 35: 39: 43: 47: 51: 55: 59) cm
(9 (10.5: 12: 14: 15.5: 17: 18.5: 20: 21.5: 23) in)

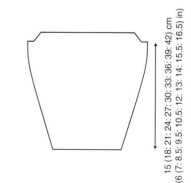

15 (18: 21: 24: 27: 30: 33: 36: 39: 42) cm
(6 (7: 8.5: 9.5: 10.5: 12: 13: 14: 15.5: 16.5) in)

DREW

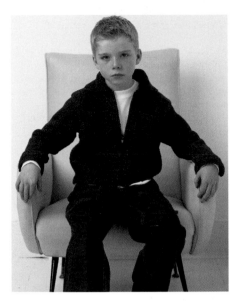

YARN

	1st	2nd	3rd	4th	5th	size
To fit age	months			years		
	0-6	6-12	1-2	2-3	3-4	
To fit chest	41	46	51	56	58	cm
	16	18	20	22	23	in
Rowan Denim						
	4	5	6	7	8	x 50gm

	6th	7th	8th	9th	10th	size
To fit age	4-5	6-7	8-9	9-10	11-12	years
To fit chest	61	66	71	76	81	cm
	24	26	28	30	32	in
Rowan Denim						
	9	10	12	13	14	x 50gm

(photographed in Nashville 225)

NEEDLES

1 pair 3¼mm (no 10) (US 3) needles
1 pair 4mm (no 8) (US 6) needles

BUTTONS – 2 x 75324 for 5th, 6th, 7th, 8th, 9th and 10th sizes only

ZIP – open-ended zip to fit

TENSION

Before washing 20 sts and 28 rows to 10 cm measured over stocking stitch using 4mm (US 6) needles.

Tension note: Denim will shrink in length when washed for the first time. Allowances have been made in this pattern for shrinkage (see size diagram for after washing measurements).

BACK

Cast on 51 (57: 61: 67: 63: 69: 73: 79: 83: 89) sts using 3¼mm (US 3) needles.
Row 1 (RS): K0 (1: 1: 0: 0: 1: 1: 0: 0: 1), *P1, K1, rep from * to last 1 (0: 0: 1: 1: 0: 0: 1: 1: 0) st, P1 (0: 0: 1: 1: 0: 0: 1: 1: 0).
Row 2: As row 1.
These 2 rows form moss st.
Work in moss st for a further 8 rows, ending with a WS row.
Change to 4mm (US 6) needles.

Beg with a K row, work in st st as folls:
5th, 6th, 7th, 8th, 9th and 10th sizes only
Inc 1 st at each end of - (-: -: -: 3rd: 3rd: 3rd: 3rd: 5th: 5th) and every foll - (-: -: -: 8th: 8th: 10th: 10th: 12th: 12th) row until there are - (-: -: -: 71: 77: 81: 87: 91: 97) sts.
All sizes
Cont straight until back measures 14.5 (15.5: 17: 18: 19: 21.5: 24: 26.5: 29: 31) cm, ending with a WS row.
Shape armholes
Cast off 3 (3: 3: 3: 4: 4: 4: 4: 4: 4) sts at beg of next 2 rows.
45 (51: 55: 61: 63: 69: 73: 79: 83: 89) sts.
Dec 1 st at each end of next 3 (3: 3: 3: 4: 4: 4: 6: 6: 6) rows. 39 (45: 49: 55: 55: 61: 65: 67: 71: 77) sts.
Cont straight until armhole measures 14.5 (15.5: 17: 18: 19: 20.5: 21.5: 23: 24: 25) cm, ending with a WS row.
Shape shoulders and back neck
Cast off 3 (4: 5: 5: 5: 6: 7: 7: 7: 8) sts at beg of next 2 rows.
33 (37: 39: 45: 45: 49: 51: 53: 57: 61) sts.
Next row (RS): Cast off 3 (4: 5: 5: 5: 6: 7: 7: 7: 8) sts, K until there are 7 (8: 8: 10: 10: 11: 10: 11: 12: 13) sts on right needle and turn, leaving rem sts on a holder.
Work each side of neck separately.
Cast off 4 sts at beg of next row.
Cast off rem 3 (4: 4: 6: 6: 7: 6: 7: 8: 9) sts.
With RS facing, rejoin yarn to rem sts, cast off centre 13 (13: 13: 15: 15: 15: 17: 17: 19: 19) sts, K to end.
Complete to match first side, reversing shapings.

POCKET LININGS (make 2)
5th, 6th, 7th, 8th, 9th and 10th sizes only
Cast on - (-: -: -: 20: 20: 22: 22: 24: 24) sts using 4mm (US 6) needles.
Beg with a K row, work in st st for 28 rows.
Break yarn and leave sts on a holder.

LEFT FRONT
Cast on 26 (29: 31: 34: 32: 35: 37: 40: 42: 45) sts using 3¼mm (US 3) needles.
Row 1 (RS): K0 (1: 1: 0: 0: 1: 1: 0: 0: 1), *P1, K1, rep from * to end.
Row 2: *K1, P1, rep from * to last 0 (1: 1: 0: 0: 1: 1: 0: 0: 1) st, K0 (1: 1: 0: 0: 1: 1: 0: 0: 1).
These 2 rows form moss st.
Work in moss st for a further 8 rows, ending with a WS row.
Change to 4mm (US 6) needles.
Next row (RS): Knit.
Next row: K1, P to end.
These 2 rows set the sts – front opening edge st worked as a K st on every row with all other sts in st st.
Keeping sts correct as set, cont as folls:
5th, 6th, 7th, 8th, 9th and 10th sizes only
Inc 1 st at beg of - (-: -: -: next: next: next: next: 3rd: 3rd) and every foll - (-: -: -: 8th: 8th: 10th: 10th: 12th: 12th) row until there are - (-: -: -: 36: 39: 41: 44: 46: 49) sts.
All sizes
Cont straight until left front matches back to beg of armhole shaping, ending with a WS row.
Shape armhole
Cast off 3 (3: 3: 3: 4: 4: 4: 4: 4: 4) sts at beg of next row.
23 (26: 28: 31: 32: 35: 37: 40: 42: 45) sts.
Work 1 row.
Dec 1 st at armhole edge of next 3 (3: 3: 3: 4: 4: 4: 6: 6: 6) rows.
20 (23: 25: 28: 28: 31: 33: 34: 36: 39) sts.

5th, 6th, 7th, 8th, 9th and 10th sizes only
Cont straight until armhole measures - (-: -: -: 6: 6: 7: 7: 8: 8) cm, ending with a WS row.
Place pocket
Next row (RS): K- (-: -: -: 4: 6: 6: 6: 6: 8), slip next - (-: -: -: 20: 20: 22: 22: 24: 24) sts onto a holder and, in their place, K across - (-: -: -: 20: 20: 22: 22: 24: 24) sts of first pocket lining, K- (-: -: -: 4: 5: 5: 6: 6: 7).
All sizes
Cont straight until 11 (11: 11: 11: 13: 13: 13: 13: 13: 13) rows less have been worked than on back to start of shoulder shaping, ending with a RS row.
Shape neck
Cast off 6 (6: 6: 7: 6: 7: 7: 8: 8) sts at beg of next row. 14 (17: 19: 21: 22: 25: 26: 27: 28: 31).
Dec 1 st at neck edge of next 3 rows, then on foll 2 (2: 2: 2: 3: 3: 3: 3: 3: 3) alt rows.
9 (12: 14: 16: 16: 19: 20: 21: 22: 25) sts.
Work 3 rows, ending with a WS row.
Shape shoulder
Cast off 3 (4: 5: 5: 5: 6: 7: 7: 7: 8) sts at beg of next and foll alt row.
Work 1 row.
Cast off rem 3 (4: 4: 6: 6: 7: 6: 7: 8: 9) sts.

RIGHT FRONT
Cast on 26 (29: 31: 34: 32: 35: 37: 40: 42: 45) sts using 3¼mm (US 3) needles.
Row 1 (RS): *K1, P1, rep from * to last 0 (1: 1: 0: 0: 1: 1: 0: 0: 1) st, K0 (1: 1: 0: 0: 1: 1: 0: 0: 1).
Row 2: K0 (1: 1: 0: 0: 1: 1: 0: 0: 1), *P1, K1, rep from * to end.
These 2 rows form moss st.
Work in moss st for a further 8 rows, ending with a WS row.
Change to 4mm (US 6) needles.
Next row (RS): Knit.
Next row: P to last st, K1.
These 2 rows set the sts – front opening edge st worked as a K st on every row with all other sts in st st.
Keeping sts correct as set, cont as folls:
5th, 6th, 7th, 8th, 9th and 10th sizes only
Inc 1 st at end of - (-: -: -: next: next: next: next: 3rd: 3rd) and every foll - (-: -: -: 8th: 8th: 10th: 10th: 12th: 12th) row until there are - (-: -: -: 36: 39: 41: 44: 46: 49) sts.
All sizes
Complete to match left front, reversing shapings and placing pocket for **5th, 6th, 7th, 8th, 9th and 10th sizes only** as folls:
Next row (RS): K- (-: -: -: 4: 5: 5: 6: 6: 7), slip next - (-: -: -: 20: 20: 22: 22: 24: 24) sts onto a holder and, in their place, K across - (-: -: -: 20: 20: 22: 22: 24: 24) sts of second pocket lining, K- (-: -: -: 4: 6: 6: 6: 6: 8).

LEFT SLEEVE
1st, 2nd, 3rd and 4th sizes only
Cast on 29 (31: 33: 35: -: -: -: -: -: -) sts using 3¼mm (US 3) needles.
Row 1 (RS): K1, *P1, K1, rep from * to end.
Row 2: As row 1.
These 2 rows form moss st.
Work in moss st for a further 6 rows, ending with a WS row.
Change to 4mm (US 6) needles.
5th, 6th, 7th, 8th, 9th and 10th sizes only
Front cuff/sleeve
Cast on - (-: -: -: 29: 29: 31: 31: 33: 33) sts using 3¼mm (US 3) needles.
Row 1 (RS): K1, *P1, K1, rep from * to end.
Row 2: As row 1.
These 2 rows form moss st.

Work in moss st for a further 4 rows, ending with a WS row.

Row 7 (RS): K1, P2tog, yrn (to make a buttonhole), moss st to end.

Work in moss st for a further 3 rows, ending with a WS row.

Change to 4mm (US 6) needles.

Next row (RS): Moss st 5 sts, K to end.

Next row: P to last 5 sts, moss st 5 sts.

These 2 rows set the sts – 5 sts still in moss st for cuff opening border and rem sts in st st.

Keeping sts correct as set, inc 1 st at end of next and foll – (–: –: –: 6th: 6th: 8th: 8th: 8th: 8th) row.

– (–: –: –: 31: 31: 33: 33: 35: 35) sts.

Work a further – (–: –: –: 5: 5: 5: 5: 7: 7) rows, ending with a WS row.

Break yarn and leave sts on a holder.

Back cuff/sleeve

Cast on – (–: –: –: 13: 13: 15: 15: 17: 17) sts using 3¼mm (US 3) needles.

Work in moss st as given for front cuff/sleeve for 10 rows, ending with a WS row.

Change to 4mm (US 6) needles.

Next row (RS): K to last 5 sts, moss st 5 sts.

Next row: Moss st 5 sts, P to end.

These 2 rows set the sts – 5 sts still in moss st for cuff opening border and rem sts in st st.

Keeping sts correct as set, inc 1 st at beg of next and foll – (–: –: –: 6th: 6th: 8th: 8th: 8th: 8th) row.

– (–: –: –: 15: 15: 17: 17: 19: 19) sts.

Work a further – (–: –: –: 5: 5: 5: 5: 7: 7) rows, ending with a WS row.

Join sections

Next row (RS): Working across sts of back cuff/sleeve, (inc in first st) – (–: –: –: 1: 1: 0: 0: 1: 1) times, K to last 5 sts, now holding WS of front cuff/sleeve against RS of back cuff/sleeve, K tog first st of front cuff/sleeve with next st of back cuff/sleeve, in same way K tog next 4 sts of front cuff/sleeve with rem 4 sts of back cuff/sleeve, working across rem sts of front cuff/sleeve, K to last – (–: –: –: 1: 1: 0: 0: 1: 1) st, (inc in last st) – (–: –: –: 1: 1: 0: 0: 1: 1) times.

– (–: –: –: 43: 43: 45: 45: 51: 51) sts.

★★All sizes

Beg with a K (K: K: K: P: P: P: P: P: P) row, now work in st st, shaping sides by inc 1 st at each end of 3rd (3rd: 3rd: 3rd: 6th: 6th: 2nd: 2nd: 8th: 8th) and every foll 4th (6th: 6th: 6th: 6th: 6th: 8th: 6th: 8th: 8th) row to 47 (39: 49: 57: 57: 65: 49: 75: 61: 59) sts, then on every foll – (4th: 4th: 4th: 4th: 4th: 6th: –: 6th: 6th) row until there are – (51: 55: 59: 63: 67: 71: –: 79: 83) sts.

Cont straight until sleeve measures 18 (21.5: 25: 29: 32.5: 36: 39.5: 43: 47: 50.5) cm, ending with a WS row.

Shape top

Cast off 3 (3: 3: 3: 4: 4: 4: 4: 4: 4) sts at beg of next 2 rows.

41 (45: 49: 53: 55: 59: 63: 67: 71: 75) sts.

Dec 1 st at each end of next and foll 3 (3: 3: 3: 4: 4: 4: 5: 5: 5) alt rows.

Work 1 row, ending with a WS row.

Cast off rem 33 (37: 41: 45: 45: 49: 53: 55: 59: 63) sts.

RIGHT SLEEVE

1st, 2nd, 3rd and 4th sizes only

Work as given for left sleeve.

5th, 6th, 7th, 8th, 9th and 10th sizes only

Back cuff/sleeve

Cast on – (–: –: –: 13: 13: 15: 15: 17: 17) sts using 3¼mm (US 3) needles.

Work in moss st as given for left sleeve for 10 rows, ending with a WS row.

Change to 4mm (US 6) needles.

Next row (RS): Moss st 5 sts, K to end.

Next row: P to last 5 sts, moss st 5 sts.

These 2 rows set the sts – 5 sts still in moss st for cuff opening border and rem sts in st st.

Keeping sts correct as set, inc 1 st at end of next and foll – (–: –: –: 6th: 6th: 8th: 8th: 8th: 8th) row.

– (–: –: –: 15: 15: 17: 17: 19: 19) sts.

Work a further – (–: –: –: 5: 5: 5: 5: 7: 7) rows, ending with a WS row.

Break yarn and leave sts on a holder.

Front cuff/sleeve

Cast on – (–: –: –: 29: 29: 31: 31: 33: 33) sts using 3¼mm (US 3) needles.

Work in moss st as given for left sleeve for 6 rows, ending with a WS row.

Row 7 (RS): Moss st to last 3 sts, yrn (to make a buttonhole), P2tog, K1.

Work in moss st for a further 3 rows, ending with a WS row.

Change to 4mm (US 6) needles.

Next row (RS): K to last 5 sts, moss st 5 sts.

Next row: Moss st 5 sts, P to end.

These 2 rows set the sts – 5 sts still in moss st for cuff opening border and rem sts in st st.

Keeping sts correct as set, inc 1 st at beg of next and foll – (–: –: –: 6th: 6th: 8th: 8th: 8th: 8th) row.

– (–: –: –: 31: 31: 33: 33: 35: 35) sts.

Work a further – (–: –: –: 5: 5: 5: 5: 7: 7) rows, ending with a WS row.

Join sections

Next row (RS): Working across sts of front cuff/sleeve, (inc in first st) – (–: –: –: 1: 1: 0: 0: 1: 1) times, K to last 5 sts, now holding RS of back cuff/sleeve against WS of front cuff/sleeve, K tog next st of front cuff/sleeve with first st of back cuff/sleeve, in same way K tog rem 4 sts of front cuff/sleeve with next 4 sts of back cuff/sleeve, working across rem sts of back cuff/sleeve, K to last – (–: –: –: 1: 1: 0: 0: 1: 1) st, (inc in last st) – (–: –: –: 1: 1: 0: 0: 1: 1) times.

– (–: –: –: 43: 43: 45: 45: 51: 51) sts.

Complete as given for left sleeve from ★★.

MAKING UP

DO NOT PRESS.

Join both shoulder seams using back stitch, or mattress st if preferred.

Collar

Cast on 63 (63: 63: 67: 71: 71: 75: 75: 79: 79) sts using 3¼mm (US 3) needles.

Work in moss st as given for left sleeve for 8 (8: 8: 8: 10: 10: 10: 12: 12: 12) cm.

Cast off in moss st.

5th, 6th, 7th, 8th, 9th and 10th sizes only

Pocket tops (both alike)

Slip – (–: –: –: 20: 20: 22: 22: 24: 24) sts left on pocket holder onto 3¼mm (US 3) needles and rejoin yarn with RS facing.

Row 1 (RS): ★K1, P1, rep from ★ to end.

Row 2: ★P1, K1, rep from ★ to end.

Rep these 2 rows twice more.

Cast off in moss st.

All sizes

Machine wash all pieces as described on the ball band before completing garment.

See information page for finishing instructions, sewing cast-on edge of collar to neck edge and setting in sleeves using the shallow set-in method. Insert zip into front opening.

1st, 2nd, 3rd, & 4th sizes

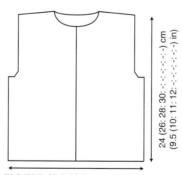

24 (26: 28: 30: -: -: -: -: -: -) cm
(9.5 (10: 11: 12: -: -: -: -: -: -) in)

25.5 (28.5: 30.5: 33.5: -: -: -: -: -: -) cm
(10 (11: 12: 13: -: -: -: -: -: -) in)

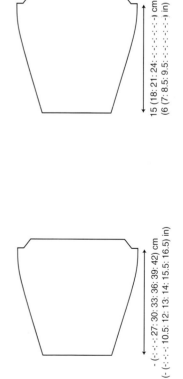

15 (18: 21: 24: -: -: -: -: -: -) cm
(6 (7: 8.5: 9.5: -: -: -: -: -: -) in)

5th, 6th, 7th, 8th, 9th & 10th sizes

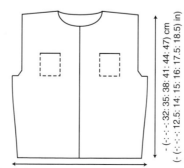

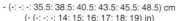

- (-: -: -: 32: 35: 38: 41: 44: 47) cm
(- (-: -: -: 12.5: 14: 15: 16: 17.5: 18.5) in)

- (-: -: -: 35.5: 38.5: 40.5: 43.5: 45.5: 48.5) cm
(- (-: -: -: 14: 15: 16: 17: 18: 19) in)

- (-: -: -: 27: 30: 33: 36: 39: 42) cm
(- (-: -: -: 10.5: 12: 13: 14: 15.5: 16.5) in)

JACK

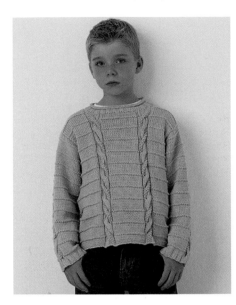

YARN

Rowan Handknit DK Cotton

	5th	6th	7th	size
To fit age	3-4	4-5	6-7	years
To fit chest	58	61	66	cm
	23	24	26	in
	7	8	9	x 50gm

	8th	9th	10th	size
To fit age	8-9	9-10	11-12	years
To fit chest	71	76	81	cm
	28	30	32	in
	11	12	14	x 50gm

(photographed in Chime 204)

NEEDLES

1 pair 3¼mm (no 10) (US 3) needles
1 pair 4mm (no 8) (US 6) needles
Cable needle

TENSION

20 sts and 28 rows to 10 cm measured over
stocking stitch using 4mm (US 6) needles.

SPECIAL ABBREVIATIONS

C8B = Cable 8 back Slip next 4 sts onto cable
needle and leave at back of work, working sts as
set by previous row, work next 4 sts, then work
4 sts from cable needle.

C8F = Cable 8 front Slip next 4 sts onto cable
needle and leave at front of work, working sts as
set by previous row, work next 4 sts, then work
4 sts from cable needle.

BACK

Cast on 81 (87: 93: 99: 105: 111) sts using
3¼mm (US 3) needles.
Row 1 (RS): K21 (23: 26: 28: 30: 32), P2, K4,
(K1, P1) twice, P2, K15 (17: 17: 19: 21: 23), P2,
(P1, K1) twice, K4, P2, K to end.
Row 2: K23 (25: 28: 30: 32: 34), P4, (K1, P1)
twice, K19 (21: 21: 23: 25: 27), (P1, K1) twice,
P4, K to end.
Rep last 2 rows twice more.
Change to 4mm (US 6) needles.
Now work in patt as folls:

Row 1 (RS): K21 (23: 26: 28: 30: 32), P2, K4,
(K1, P1) twice, P2, K15 (17: 17: 19: 21: 23), P2,
(P1, K1) twice, K4, P2, K to end.
Row 2: P21 (23: 26: 28: 30: 32), K2, P4, (K1, P1)
twice, K2, P15 (17: 17: 19: 21: 23), K2, (P1, K1)
twice, P4, K2, P to end.
Rows 3 and 4: As rows 1 and 2.
Row 5: K23 (25: 28: 30: 32: 34), C8B, P19 (21:
21: 23: 25: 27), C8F, P to end.
Row 6: P21 (23: 26: 28: 30: 32), K2, (K1, P1)
twice, P4, K2, P15 (17: 17: 19: 21: 23), K2, P4,
(P1, K1) twice, K2, P to end.
Row 7: K21 (23: 26: 28: 30: 32), P2, (K1, P1)
twice, K4, P2, K15 (17: 17: 19: 21: 23), P2, K4,
(P1, K1) twice, P2, K to end.
Rows 8 to 13: As rows 6 and 7, 3 times.
Row 14: As row 6.
Row 15: As row 5.
Row 16: As row 2.
Rows 17 to 20: As rows 1 and 2, twice.
These 20 rows form patt.
Cont straight in patt until back measures 16 (20:
23: 26: 28: 30) cm, ending with a WS row.

Shape armholes
Keeping patt correct, cast off 4 sts at beg of next
2 rows. 73 (79: 85: 91: 97: 103) sts.
Dec 1 st at each end of next 6 rows.
61 (67: 73: 79: 85: 91) sts.
Cont straight until armhole measures 17 (18: 19:
20: 21: 22) cm, ending with a WS row.

Shape shoulders and back neck
Cast off 4 (5: 6: 7: 8: 8) sts at beg of next 2 rows.
53 (57: 61: 65: 69: 75) sts.
Next row (RS): Cast off 4 (5: 6: 7: 8: 8) sts, patt
until there are 9 (9: 10: 10: 11: 13) sts on right
needle and turn, leaving rem sts on a holder.
Work each side of neck separately.
Cast off 4 sts at beg of next row.
Cast off rem 5 (5: 6: 6: 7: 9) sts.
With RS facing, rejoin yarn to rem sts, cast off
centre 27 (29: 29: 31: 31: 33) sts, patt to end.
Complete to match first side, reversing shapings.

FRONT

Work as given for back until 12 (12: 12: 14: 14:
14) rows less have been worked than on back to
start of shoulder shaping, ending with a WS row.

Shape neck
Next row (RS): Patt 19 (21: 24: 27: 30: 32) sts
and turn, leaving rem sts on a holder.
Work each side of neck separately.
Dec 1 st at neck edge of next 4 rows, then on foll
2 (2: 2: 3: 3: 3) alt rows. 13 (15: 18: 20: 23: 25) sts.
Work 3 rows, ending with a WS row.

Shape shoulder
Cast off 4 (5: 6: 7: 8: 8) sts at beg of next and foll
alt row.
Work 1 row. Cast off rem 5 (5: 6: 6: 7: 9) sts.
With RS facing, rejoin yarn to rem sts, cast off
centre 23 (25: 25: 25: 25: 27) sts, patt to end.
Complete to match first side, reversing shapings.

LEFT SLEEVE

Cast on 48 (50: 52: 54: 56: 58) sts using 3¼mm
(US 3) needles.
Row 1 (RS): P0 (1: 0: 0: 0: 1), K2 (2: 0: 1: 2: 2),
(P2, K2) 4 (4: 5: 5: 5: 5) times, P2, (P1, K1) twice,
K4, P2, (K2, P2) 4 (4: 5: 5: 5: 5) times, K2 (2: 0: 1:
2: 2), P0 (1: 0: 0: 0: 1).
Row 2: K0 (1: 0: 0: 0: 1), P2 (2: 0: 1: 2: 2), (K2,
P2) 4 (4: 5: 5: 5: 5) times, K2, P4, (K1, P1) twice,
K2, (P2, K2) 4 (4: 5: 5: 5: 5) times, P2 (2: 0: 1: 2:
2), K0 (1: 0: 0: 0: 1).
Rep last 2 rows twice more.
Change to 4mm (US 6) needles.
Now work in patt as folls:
Row 1 (RS): K18 (19: 20: 21: 22: 23), P2,
(P1, K1) twice, K4, P2, K to end.
Row 2: P18 (19: 20: 21: 22: 23), K2, P4,
(K1, P1) twice, K2, P to end.
Rows 3 and 4: As rows 1 and 2.
Row 5: P20 (21: 22: 23: 24: 25), C8F, P to end.
Row 6: P18 (19: 20: 21: 22: 23), K2, (K1, P1)
twice, P4, K2, P to end.
These 6 rows set position of patt as given for back.
****Keeping patt correct, inc 1 st at each end of
next and every foll 4th (4th: 4th: 6th: 6th: 6th)
row to 68 (64: 60: 60: 88: 88) sts, then on every
foll 6th (6th: 6th: 6th: -: 8th) row until there are
72 (76: 80: 84: -: 92) sts, taking inc sts into patt.
Cont straight until sleeve measures 24 (28: 32:
36: 40: 43) cm, ending with a WS row.

Shape top
Keeping patt correct, cast off 4 sts at beg of next
2 rows. 64 (68: 72: 76: 80: 84) sts.
Dec 1 st at each end of next and foll 5 alt rows.
Work 1 row, ending with a WS row.
Cast off rem 52 (56: 60: 64: 68: 72) sts.

RIGHT SLEEVE

Cast on 48 (50: 52: 54: 56: 58) sts using 3¼mm
(US 3) needles.
Row 1 (RS): P0 (1: 0: 0: 0: 1), K2 (2: 0: 1: 2: 2),
(P2, K2) 4 (4: 5: 5: 5: 5) times, P2, K4, (K1, P1)
twice, P2, (K2, P2) 4 (4: 5: 5: 5: 5) times, K2 (2: 0:
1: 2: 2), P0 (1: 0: 0: 0: 1).
Row 2: K0 (1: 0: 0: 0: 1), P2 (2: 0: 1: 2: 2),
(K2, P2) 4 (4: 5: 5: 5: 5) times, K2, (P1, K1)
twice, P4, K2, (P2, K2) 4 (4: 5: 5: 5: 5) times,
P2 (2: 0: 1: 2: 2), K0 (1: 0: 0: 0: 1).
Rep last 2 rows twice more.
Change to 4mm (US 6) needles.
Now work in patt as folls:
Row 1 (RS): K18 (19: 20: 21: 22: 23), P2, K4,
(K1, P1) twice, P2, K to end.
Row 2: P18 (19: 20: 21: 22: 23), K2, (K1, P1)
twice, P4, K2, P to end.
Rows 3 and 4: As rows 1 and 2.
Row 5: P20 (21: 22: 23: 24: 25), C8B, P to end.
Row 6: P18 (19: 20: 21: 22: 23), K2, P4,
(P1, K1) twice, K2, P to end.
These 6 rows set position of patt as given for back.
Complete to match left sleeve from **.

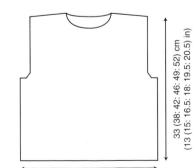

33 (38: 42: 46: 49: 52) cm
(13 (15: 16.5: 18: 19.5: 20.5) in)

36.5 (39.5: 42.5: 45.5: 48.5: 51.5) cm
(14.5 (15.5: 16.5: 18: 19: 20.5) in)

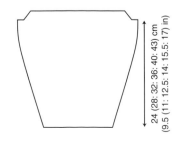

24 (28: 32: 36: 40: 43) cm
(9.5 (11: 12.5: 14: 15.5: 17) in)

MAKING UP

PRESS as described on the information page. Join right shoulder seam using back stitch, or mattress st if preferred.

Neckband

With RS facing and using 3¼mm (US 3) needles, pick up and knit 15 (15: 15: 18: 18: 18) sts down left side of neck, 23 (25: 25: 25: 25: 27) sts from front, 15 (15: 15: 18: 18: 18) sts up right side of neck, then 35 (37: 37: 39: 39: 41) sts from back. 88 (92: 92: 100: 100: 104) sts.

Row 1 (WS): ★K2, P2, rep from ★ to end.

Rep last row 5 times more, ending with a RS row.

Beg with a P row, work in st st for 5 rows.

Cast off knitwise.

See information page for finishing instructions, setting in sleeves using the shallow set-in method.

SID

YARN

	1st	2nd	3rd	4th	5th	size
To fit age	months		years			
	0-6	6-12	1-2	2-3	3-4	
To fit chest	41	46	51	56	58	cm
	16	18	20	22	23	in

Rowan Big Wool

3   3   4   4   5   x100gm

(photographed in White Hot 001)

NEEDLES

1 pair 15mm (US 19) needles

BUTTONS – 2 x 75336

TENSION

7½ sts and 10 rows to 10 cm measured over stocking stitch using 15mm (US 19) needles.

BACK and FRONTS (worked in one piece to armholes)

Cast on 51 (55: 59: 63: 67) sts using 15mm (US 19) needles.

Work in garter st for 3 rows, ending with **wrong** side row.

Next row (RS): Knit.

Next row: K3, P to last 3 sts, K3.

These 2 rows set the sts – 3 st garter st border at each end of row and st st between.

Keeping sts correct, cont as folls:

Work a further 8 (10: 12: 14: 16) rows, ending with a WS row. Work should measure approx 13 (15: 17: 19: 21) cm.

Divide for armholes

Next row (RS): K13 (14: 15: 16: 17) and slip these sts onto a holder for right front, cast off next 2 sts, K until there are 21 (23: 25: 27: 29) sts on right needle after cast-off and slip these sts onto another holder for back, cast off next 2 sts, K to end.

Work on this last set of 13 (14: 15: 16: 17) sts for left front as folls:

Work 3 rows, ending with a WS row.

Shape for collar

Row 1 (RS): K to last 3 sts, M1, K3.
14 (15: 16: 17: 18) sts.

Row 2: K4, P to end.

Row 3: Knit.

Row 4: K5, P to end.

Row 5: K to last 6 sts, M1, K6.
15 (16: 17: 18: 19) sts.

Row 6: K7, P to end.

Row 7: Knit.

Row 8: K8, P to end.

Row 9: K to last 8 sts, M1, K8.
16 (17: 18: 19: 20) sts.

Row 10: K9, P to end.

3rd, 4th and 5th sizes only

Row 11: Knit.

Row 12: K10, P to end.

Rep last 2 rows - (-: 0: 0: 1) times more.

All sizes

Armhole should measure 14 (14: 16: 16: 18) cm.

Shape shoulder

Next row (RS): K7 (8: 8: 9: 10) and slip these sts onto a holder for left shoulder seam, K to end. 9 (9: 10: 10: 10) sts.

Work 9 (9: 11: 11: 11) rows in garter st on these 9 (9: 10: 10: 10) sts.

Cast off.

Shape back

With WS facing, rejoin yarn to 21 (23: 25: 27: 29) sts left on back holder.

Work 13 (13: 15: 15: 17) rows, ending with a WS row.

Shape shoulders

Next row (RS): K7 (8: 8: 9: 10) and slip these sts onto a holder for right shoulder seam, cast off next 7 (7: 9: 9: 9) sts for back neck, K to end and slip this last set of 7 (8: 8: 9: 10) sts onto another holder for left shoulder seam.

Shape right front

With WS facing, rejoin yarn to 13 (14: 15: 16: 17) sts left on right front holder and work 3 rows, ending with a WS row.

Shape for collar

Row 1 (RS): K3, M1, K to end.
14 (15: 16: 17: 18) sts.

Row 2: P to last 4 sts, K4.

Row 3: Knit.

Row 4: P to last 5 sts, K5.

Row 5: K6, M1, K to end.
15 (16: 17: 18: 19) sts.

Row 6: P to last 7 sts, K7.

Row 7: Knit.

Row 8: P to last 8 sts, K8.

Row 9: K8, M1, K to end. 16 (17: 18: 19: 20) sts.

Row 10: P to last 9 sts, K9.

3rd, 4th and 5th sizes only

Row 11: Knit.

Row 12: P to last 10 sts, K10.

Rep last 2 rows - (-: 0: 0: 1) times more.

All sizes

Work 1 row, ending with a RS row.

Shape shoulder

Break yarn and slip last 7 (8: 8: 9: 10) sts of last row onto a holder for right shoulder seam.

Rejoin yarn to rem 9 (9: 10: 10: 10) sts with WS facing and K to end.

Work a further 8 (8: 10: 10: 10) rows in garter st on these 9 (9: 10: 10: 10) sts.

Cast off.

SLEEVES

Cast on 13 (13: 14: 14: 15) sts using 15mm (US 19) needles.

Work in garter st for 3 rows, ending with **wrong** side row.

Beg with a K row, cont in st st as folls:

Inc 1 st at each end of next and every foll alt (4th: 4th: 4th: 4th) row to 17 (21: 24: 22: 25) sts, then on foll 4th (-: -: 6th: 6th) row.
21 (21: 24: 24: 27) sts.

Work a further 3 (3: 3: 5: 5) rows, ending with a WS row. Work should measure approx 17 (19: 23: 27: 31) cm.

Cast off.

MAKING UP

PRESS as described on the information page.

Join shoulder seams as folls: With WS together and working with RS of front towards you, join shoulder seams by casting off 7 (8: 8: 9: 10) sts of front shoulder together with corresponding set of back shoulder sts from holders.

Join centre back seam of collar, then slip stitch collar in position to back neck.

Attach 2 buttons to left front – top button to come just below start of front slope shaping, and other button to come midway between this button and cast-on edge. To fasten buttons, push them through knitting of right front, enlarging a stitch if required.

See information page for finishing instructions, setting in sleeves using the straight cast-off method.

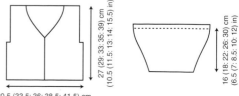

30.5 (33.5: 36: 38.5: 41.5) cm
(12 (13: 14: 15: 16.5) in)

27 (29: 33: 35: 39) cm
(10.5 (11.5: 13: 14: 15.5) in)

16 (18: 22: 26: 30) cm
(6.5 (7: 8.5: 10: 12) in)

Toby

YARN

	2nd	3rd	4th	5th	6th	size
	months		years			
To fit age	6-12	1-2	2-3	3-4	4-5	
To fit chest	46	51	56	58	61	cm
	18	20	22	23	24	in
Rowan Wool Cotton						
A Clear 941	3	4	5	6	7	x 50gm
B Gypsy 910	1	1	1	1	1	x 50gm

NEEDLES

1 pair 3¼mm (no 10) (US 3) needles
1 pair 4mm (no 8) (US 6) needles

TENSION

22 sts and 30 rows to 10 cm measured over stocking stitch using 4mm (US 6) needles.

BACK

Cast on 71 (77: 83: 89: 95) sts using 3¼mm (US 3) needles and yarn A.
Row 1 (RS): P1, *K3, P3, rep from * to last 4 sts, K3, P1.
Row 2: K1, *P3, K3, rep from * to last 4 sts, P3, K1.
These 2 rows form rib.
Work in rib for a further 6 rows, ending with a WS row.
Change to 4mm (US 6) needles.
Beg with a K row, cont in st st as folls:
Work 6 (8: 10: 12: 14) rows, ending with a WS row.**

Place first spot

Join in yarn B and place spot motif as folls:
Next row (RS): K9 (11: 13: 15: 17), starting with chart row 1 and using the INTARSIA method as described on the information page, work across 21 sts from spot chart, K41 (45: 49: 53: 57).
Next row: P41 (45: 49: 53: 57), work across 21 sts from chart, P9 (11: 13: 15: 17).
Cont working from chart until chart row 28 has been completed **and at same time** when back measures 11 (13: 16: 19: 20) cm, ending with a WS row, shape armholes as folls:

Shape armholes

Cast off 5 sts at beg of next 2 rows.
61 (67: 73: 79: 85) sts.

Work a further 2 (4: 6: 8: 10) rows, ending with a WS row.

Place second spot

Join in yarn B and place spot motif as folls:
Next row (RS): K36 (40: 44: 48: 52), starting with chart row 1 and using the INTARSIA method as described on the information page, work across 21 sts from spot chart, K4 (6: 8: 10: 12).
Next row: P4 (6: 8: 10: 12), work across 21 sts from chart, P36 (40: 44: 48: 52).
Cont working from chart until chart row 28 has been completed.
Cont straight until armhole measures 13 (15: 16: 17: 18) cm, ending with a WS row.

Shape shoulders and back neck

Cast off 6 (7: 7: 8: 9) sts at beg of next 2 rows.
49 (53: 59: 63: 67) sts.
Next row (RS): Cast off 6 (7: 7: 8: 9) sts, K until there are 10 (10: 12: 12: 12) sts on right needle and turn, leaving rem sts on a holder.
Work each side of neck separately.
Cast off 4 sts at beg of next row.
Cast off rem 6 (6: 8: 8: 8) sts.

2nd size only

With RS facing, slip centre 17 (-: -: -: -) sts onto a holder, rejoin yarn to rem sts, K to end.

3rd, 4th, 5th and 6th sizes only

With RS facing, rejoin yarn to rem sts, cast off centre - (19: 21: 23: 25) sts, K to end.

All sizes

Complete to match first side, reversing shapings.

FRONT

Work as given for back to **.

Place first spot

Join in yarn B and place spot motif as folls:
Next row (RS): K41 (45: 49: 53: 57), starting with chart row 1 and using the INTARSIA method as described on the information page, work across 21 sts from spot chart, K9 (11: 13: 15: 17).
Next row: P9 (11: 13: 15: 17), work across 21 sts from chart, P41 (45: 49: 53: 57).
Cont working from chart until chart row 28 has been completed **and at same time** when front matches back to beg of armhole shaping, ending with a WS row, shape armholes as folls:

Shape armholes

Cast off 5 sts at beg of next 2 rows.
61 (67: 73: 79: 85) sts.
Work a further 2 (4: 6: 8: 10) rows, ending with a WS row.

Place second spot

Join in yarn B and place spot motif as folls:
Next row (RS): K4 (6: 8: 10: 12), starting with chart row 1 and using the INTARSIA method as described on the information page, work across 21 sts from spot chart, K36 (40: 44: 48: 52).

Next row: P36 (40: 44: 48: 52), work across 21 sts from chart, P4 (6: 8: 10: 12).
Cont working from chart until chart row 28 has been completed **and at same time** when 10 (10: 10: 12: 12) rows less have been worked than on back to start of shoulder shaping, ending with a WS row, shape neck as folls:

Shape neck

Next row (RS): K24 (26: 28: 31: 33) and turn, leaving rem sts on a holder.
Work each side of neck separately.
Dec 1 st at neck edge of next 4 rows, then on foll 2 (2: 2: 3: 3) alt rows. 18 (20: 22: 24: 26) sts.
Work 1 row, ending with a WS row.

Shape shoulder

Cast off 6 (7: 7: 8: 9) sts at beg of next and foll alt row.
Work 1 row.
Cast off rem 6 (6: 8: 8: 8) sts.

2nd size only

With RS facing, slip centre 13 (-: -: -: -) sts onto a holder, rejoin yarn to rem sts, K to end.

3rd, 4th, 5th and 6th sizes only

With RS facing, rejoin yarn to rem sts, cast off centre - (15: 17: 17: 19) sts, K to end.

All sizes

Complete to match first side, reversing shapings.

SLEEVES

Spot motifs on sleeves are in different places. To position motifs, place marker on centre st. On left sleeve, work 4 (4: 6: 6: 8) rows then place spot motif as folls: work to within 6 sts of marked centre st, work next 21 sts as row 1 of spot motif, work to end. On right sleeve, work 12 (20: 26: 32: 38) rows then place spot motif as folls: work to within 16 sts of marked centre st, work next 21 sts as row 1 of spot motif, work to end. Once all 28 rows of spot motifs have been completed, work sts above motif in st st using yarn A.
Cast on 39 (41: 43: 45: 47) sts using 3¼mm (US 3) needles and yarn A.

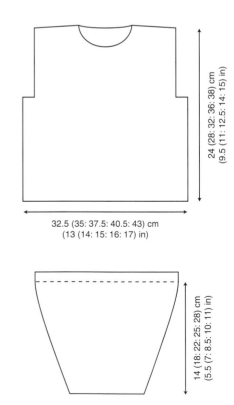

24 (28: 32: 36: 38) cm
(9.5 (11: 12.5: 14: 15) in)

32.5 (35: 37.5: 40.5: 43) cm
(13 (14: 15: 16: 17) in)

14 (18: 22: 25: 28) cm
(5.5 (7: 8.5: 10: 11) in)

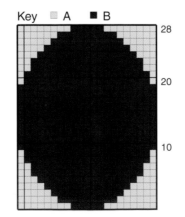

Key ☐ A ■ B

28

20

10

Row 1 (RS): K3 (1: 2: 3: 1), *P3, K3, rep from * to last 6 (4: 5: 6: 4) sts, P3, K3 (1: 2: 3: 1).
Row 2: P3 (1: 2: 3: 1), *K3, P3, rep from * to last 6 (4: 5: 6: 4) sts, K3, P3 (1: 2: 3: 1).
These 2 rows form rib.
Work in rib for a further 6 rows, ending with a WS row.
Change to 4mm (US 6) needles.
Beg with a K row and placing spot motifs as detailed above, cont in st st as folls:
Inc 1 st at each end of next and every foll 4th row to 53 (57: 69: 73: 73) sts, then on every foll alt (alt: alt: 6th: 6th) row until there are 57 (67: 71: 75: 79) sts.
Cont straight until sleeve measures 16 (20: 24: 27: 30) cm, ending with a WS row.
Cast off.

MAKING UP
PRESS as described on the information page.
Join right shoulder seam using back stitch, or mattress st if preferred.
Neckband
With RS facing, using 3¼mm (US 3) needles and yarn A, pick up and knit 14 (14: 14: 16: 17) sts down left side of neck, 14 (14: 17: 17: 19) sts from front, 14 (14: 14: 16: 17) sts up right side of neck, then 27 (27: 30: 32: 34) sts from back. 69 (69: 75: 81: 87) sts.
Row 1 (WS): P3, *K3, P3, rep from * to end.
Row 2: K3, *P3, K3, rep from * to end.
Rep last 2 rows 2 (2: 3: 3: 3) times more.
Cast off **loosely** in rib.
See information page for finishing instructions, setting in sleeves using the square set-in method.

FAYE

YARN

	7th	8th	9th	10th	size
To fit age	6-7	8-9	9-10	11-12	years
To fit chest	66	71	76	81	cm
	26	28	30	32	in
Rowan All Seasons Cotton					
A Valour	181	2	2	2	2	x 50gm
Rowan Wool Cotton					
B Tulip	944	2	3	3	4	x 50gm

NEEDLES
1 pair 3¾mm (no 9) (US 5) needles
1 pair 4mm (no 8) (US 6) needles

TENSION
22 sts and 30 rows to 10 cm measured over stocking stitch using 4mm (US 6) needles and yarn B.

Pattern note: As row end edges of armhole form actual finished edges of garment, it is important these edges are kept neat. Therefore avoid joining in new balls of yarn at these edges.

BACK
Cast on 42 (47: 47: 52) sts using 4mm (US 6) needles and yarn A.
Row 1 (RS): P2, *K3, P2, rep from * to end.
Row 2: K2, *P3, K2, rep from * to end.
These 2 rows form rib.

Work in rib for a further 18 rows, ending with a WS row.
Break off yarn A and join in yarn B.
Next row (inc) (RS): K4 (1: 2: 5), M1, *K3 (4: 3: 3), M1, rep from * to last 5 (2: 3: 5) sts, K to end. 54 (59: 62: 67) sts.
Beg with a **purl** row, cont in st st as folls:
Work 1 row.
Next row (inc) (RS): K2, M1, K to last 2 sts, M1, K2.
Working all increases as set by last row, inc 1 st at each end of every foll 6th (8th: 8th: 8th) row until there are 64 (69: 74: 79) sts.
Cont straight until back measures 20 (22: 24: 25) cm, ending with a WS row.
Shape armholes
Cast off 2 (3: 3: 4) sts at beg of next 2 rows. 60 (63: 68: 71) sts.
Row 1 (RS): K2, P1, P2tog, K to last 5 sts, P2tog tbl, P1, K1, pick up loop lying between needles and place loop on right needle (**note:** this loop does NOT count as a st), sl last st knitwise.
Row 2: P tog first st and the loop, P1, K1, K2tog tbl, P to last 5 sts, K2tog, K1, P1, pick up loop lying between needles and place loop on right needle (**note:** this loop does NOT count as a st), sl last st purlwise.
Row 3: K tog tbl first st and the loop, K1, P1, P2tog, K to last 5 sts, P2tog tbl, P1, K1, pick up loop lying between needles and place loop on right needle, sl last st knitwise.
Row 4: P tog first st and the loop, P1, K2, P to last 4 sts, K2, P1, pick up loop lying between needles and place loop on right needle, sl last st purlwise.
Rep rows 3 and 4, 0 (0: 1: 1) times more. 54 (57: 60: 63) sts.
Next row (RS): K tog tbl first st and the loop, K1, P2, K to last 4 sts, P2, K1, pick up loop lying between needles and place loop on right needle, sl last st knitwise.
Next row: P tog first st and the loop, P1, K2, P to last 4 sts, K2, P1, pick up loop lying between needles and place loop on right needle, sl last st purlwise.
Last 2 rows form slip st edging.
Cont straight as set until armhole measures 13 (14: 15: 16) cm, ending with a WS row.
Shape shoulders and back neck
Cast off 4 (5: 5: 5) sts at beg of next 2 rows. 46 (47: 50: 53) sts.
Next row (RS): Cast off 4 (5: 5: 5) sts, K until there are 9 (8: 9: 10) sts on right needle and turn, leaving rem sts on a holder.
Work each side of neck separately.
Cast off 4 sts at beg of next row.
Cast off rem 5 (4: 5: 6) sts.

With RS facing, rejoin yarn to rem sts, cast off centre 20 (21: 22: 23) sts, K to end.
Complete to match first side, reversing shapings.

FRONT
Work as given for back until 12 (12: 14: 14) rows less have been worked than on back to start of shoulder shaping, ending with a WS row.
Shape neck
Next row (RS): Patt 20 (21: 22: 23) sts and turn, leaving rem sts on a holder.
Work each side of neck separately.
Dec 1 st at neck edge of next 4 rows, then on foll 3 alt rows. 13 (14: 15: 16) sts.
Work 1 (1: 3: 3) rows, ending with a WS row.
Shape shoulder
Cast off 4 (5: 5: 5) sts at beg of next and foll alt row.
Work 1 row.
Cast off rem 5 (4: 5: 6) sts.
With RS facing, rejoin yarn to rem sts, cast off centre 14 (15: 16: 17) sts, patt to end.
Complete to match first side, reversing shapings.

MAKING UP
PRESS as described on the information page.
Join right shoulder seam using back stitch, or mattress st if preferred.
Neckband
With RS facing, using 3¾mm (US 5) needles and yarn A, pick up and knit 16 (16: 18: 18) sts down left side of neck, 14 (14: 17: 17) sts from front, 16 (16: 18: 18) sts up right side of neck, then 27 (27: 30: 30) sts from back. 73 (73: 83: 83) sts.
Row 1 (WS): P3, *K2, P3, rep from * to end.
Row 2: K3, *P2, K3, rep from * to end.
These 2 rows form rib.
Cont in rib until collar measures 7 cm.
Change to 4mm (US 8) needles and cont in rib until collar measures 18 (18: 20: 20) cm.
Cast off **loosely** in rib.
See information page for finishing instructions, reversing collar seam for turn-back.

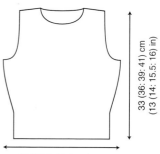

33 (36: 39: 41) cm
(13 (14: 15.5: 16) in)

29 (31.5: 33.5: 36) cm
(11.5 (12.5: 13: 14) in)

LOTTIE

YARN

To fit age	1st	2nd	3rd	4th	5th	size
	months		years			
	0-6	6-12	1-2	2-3	3-4	
To fit chest	41	46	51	56	58	cm
	16	18	20	22	23	in
Rowan 4 ply Soft						
	3	3	4	4	5	x 50gm

(photographed in Wink 377)
Oddment of same yarn in contrast colour (Buzz 375) for optional flower centre

NEEDLES

1 pair 2¾mm (no 12) (US 2) needles
1 pair 3¼mm (no 10) (US 3) needles

BUTTONS – 1 x 75333

TENSION

28 sts and 36 rows to 10 cm measured over stocking stitch using 3¼mm (US 3) needles.

BACK

Cast on 71 (77: 83: 89: 95) sts using 2¾mm (US 2) needles.
Knit 3 rows, ending with a RS row.
Now work in moss st as folls:
Row 1 (WS): K1, *P1, K1, rep from * to end.
Row 2: As row 1.
These 2 rows form moss st.
Work in moss st for a further 3 rows, ending with a WS row.
Change to 3¼mm (US 3) needles.
Beg with a K row, cont in st st as folls:
Cont straight until back measures 11 (14: 17: 20: 23) cm, ending with a WS row.
Shape raglan armholes
Cast off 5 sts at beg of next 2 rows.
61 (67: 73: 79: 85) sts.
Next row (RS): P2, K2tog, K to last 4 sts, K2tog tbl, P2.
Next row: K2, P2 tog tbl, P to last 4 sts, P2tog, K2.
Working all raglan decreases as set by last 2 rows, dec 1 st at each end of next 5 rows, then on every foll alt row until 21 (23: 25: 27: 29) sts rem, then on foll row, ending with a WS row.
Cast off rem 19 (21: 23: 25: 27) sts.

LEFT FRONT

Cast on 39 (41: 45: 47: 51) sts using 2¾mm (US 2) needles.
Knit 3 rows, ending with a RS row.
Work in moss st as given for back for 4 rows, ending with a RS row.
Next row (WS): Moss st 5 sts and slip these sts onto a holder for left front band, M1, moss st to last 0 (1: 0: 1: 0) st, (inc in last st) 0 (1: 0: 1: 0) times. 35 (38: 41: 44: 47) sts.
Change to 3¼mm (US 3) needles.
Beg with a K row, cont in st st as folls:
Cont straight until left front matches back to beg of raglan armhole shaping, ending with a WS row.
Shape raglan armhole
Cast off 5 sts at beg of next row.
30 (33: 36: 39: 42) sts.
Work 1 row.
Working all raglan decreases as set by back, dec 1 st at raglan edge of next 7 rows, then on every foll alt row until 15 (16: 18: 19: 20) sts rem, ending with a RS row.
Shape neck
Cast off 5 (6: 6: 7: 8) sts at beg of next row.
10 (10: 12: 12: 12) sts.
Dec 1 st at neck edge of next 4 (4: 5: 5: 5) rows **and at same time** dec 1 st at raglan edge of next and every foll alt row. 4 sts.
Work 0 (0: 1: 1: 1) row, ending with a WS row.
Next row (RS): (P2tog) twice.
Next row: K2.
Next row: P2tog and fasten off.

RIGHT FRONT

Cast on 39 (41: 45: 47: 51) sts using 2¾mm (US 2) needles.
Knit 3 rows, ending with a RS row.
Work in moss st as given for back for 4 rows, ending with a RS row.
Next row (WS): (Inc in first st) 0 (1: 0: 1: 0) times, moss st to last 5 sts, M1 and turn, leaving last 5 sts on a holder for right front band. 35 (38: 41: 44: 47) sts.
Change to 3¼mm (US 3) needles.
Beg with a K row, cont in st st and complete to match left front, reversing shapings.

SLEEVES

Cast on 39 (41: 43: 45: 47) sts using 2¾mm (US 2) needles.
Knit 3 rows, ending with a RS row.
Work in moss st as given for back for 5 rows, inc 1 st at each end of 4th of these rows and ending with a WS row. 41 (43: 45: 47: 49) sts.
Change to 3¼mm (US 3) needles.
Beg with a K row, cont in st st, shaping sides by inc 1 st at each end of 3rd (3rd: 5th: 5th: 7th) and every foll 4th (4th: 6th: 6th: 8th) row to 51 (61: 53: 67: 53) sts, then on every foll alt (-: 4th: 4th: 6th) row until there are 57 (-: 65: 69: 73) sts.
Cont straight until sleeve measures 11 (14: 18: 22: 26) cm, ending with a WS row.
Shape raglan
Cast off 5 sts at beg of next 2 rows.
47 (51: 55: 59: 63) sts.
Working all raglan decreases as set by back and fronts, dec 1 st at each end of next and every foll alt row until 17 sts rem.
Work 1 row, ending with a WS row.
Left sleeve only
Dec 1 st at each end of next row, then cast off 4 sts at beg of foll row. 11 sts.
Dec 1 st at beg of next row, then cast off 5 sts at beg of foll row. 5 sts.

Right sleeve only

Cast off 5 sts at beg and dec 1 st at end of next row. 11 sts.
Work 1 row.
Rep last 2 rows once more. 5 sts.
Both sleeves
Cast off rem 5 sts.

MAKING UP

PRESS as described on the information page.
Join raglan seams using back stitch, or mattress st if preferred.
Left front band
Slip 5 sts left on holder onto 2¾mm (US 2) needles and rejoin yarn with RS facing.
Cont in moss st as set until band, when slightly stretched, fits up left front to neck shaping, ending with a WS row.
Break yarn and leave sts on a holder.
Right front band
Slip 5 sts left on holder onto 2¾mm (US 2) needles and rejoin yarn with WS facing.
Cont in moss st as set until band, when slightly stretched, fits up right front to neck shaping, ending with a WS row.
Do NOT break off yarn.
Slip stitch bands in position.
Neckband
With RS facing and using 2¾mm (US 2) needles, moss st 5 sts from right front band, pick up and knit 12 (13: 15: 16: 17) sts up right side of neck, 15 sts from right sleeve, 19 (21: 23: 25: 27) sts from back, 15 sts from left sleeve, and 12 (13: 15: 16: 17) sts down left side of neck, then moss st 5 sts from left front band.
83 (87: 93: 97: 101) sts.
Work in moss st as set by front bands for 2 rows.
Row 3 (WS): Moss st to last 3 sts, yrn (to make a buttonhole), work 2 tog, moss st 1 st.
Work in moss st for a further 2 rows.
Cast off in moss st.
Flower (optional)
Following instructions given for flower of Alice bag and using 2¾mm (US 2) needles, make flower using main colour yarn for petals and oddment of contrast colour for centre. Attach flower as in photograph.
See information page for finishing instructions.

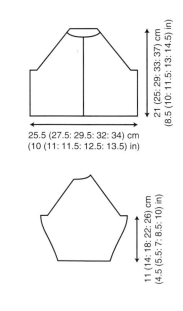

25.5 (27.5: 29.5: 32: 34) cm
(10 (11: 11.5: 12.5: 13.5) in)

21 (25: 29: 33: 37) cm
(8.5 (10: 11.5: 13: 14.5) in)

11 (14: 18: 22: 26) cm
(4.5 (5.5: 7: 8.5: 10) in)

WILL

YARN

Rowan Wool Cotton

	6th	7th	8th	9th	10th size
To fit age	4-5	6-7	8-9	9-10	11-12years
To fit chest	61	66	71	76	81 cm
	24	26	28	30	32 in
A Dpst Olive907	5	6	7	8	9 x 50gm
B Mango 950	1	1	1	2	2 x 50gm

NEEDLES

1 pair 3¼mm (no 10) (US 3) needles
1 pair 3¾mm (no 9) (US 5) needles
1 pair 4mm (no 8) (US 6) needles

ZIP – zip to fit

TENSION

22 sts and 30 rows to 10 cm measured over stocking stitch using 4mm (US 6) needles.

BACK

Cast on 89 (95: 101: 107: 113) sts using 3¼mm (US 3) needles and yarn A.
Row 1 (RS): K0 (2: 0: 0: 3), P2 (3: 0: 3: 3), *K5, P3, rep from * to last 7 (2: 5: 0: 3) sts, K5 (2: 5: 0: 3), P2 (0: 0: 0: 0).
Row 2: P0 (2: 0: 0: 3), K2 (3: 0: 3: 3), *P5, K3, rep from * to last 7 (2: 5: 0: 3) sts, P5 (2: 5: 0: 3), K2 (0: 0: 0: 0).
These 2 rows form rib.
Work in rib for a further 14 rows, ending with a WS row.
Change to 4mm (US 6) needles.
Beg with a K row, cont in st st as folls:
Work straight until back measures 21 (24: 26: 28: 30) cm, ending with a WS row.
Shape raglan armholes
Cast off 5 sts at beg of next 2 rows.
79 (85: 91: 97: 103) sts.
Dec 1 st at each end of next 5 rows, then on every foll alt row until 29 (31: 33: 35: 37) sts rem.
Work 1 row, ending with a WS row. Cast off.

FRONT

Work as given for back until 67 (69: 73: 75: 77) sts rem in raglan shaping.
Work 1 row, ending with a WS row.

Divide for front opening

Next row (RS): K2tog, K31 (32: 34: 35: 36) and turn, leaving rem sts on a holder.
32 (33: 35: 36: 37) sts.
Work each side of neck separately.
Next row (WS): K1, P to end.
Next row: K2tog, K to end.
Last 2 rows set front opening edge st worked as a K st on every row.
Keeping sts correct as set, dec 1 st at raglan edge on 2nd and every foll alt row until 21 (22: 24: 25: 26) sts rem.
Work 1 row, ending with a WS row.
Shape neck
Next row (RS): K2tog, K9 (9: 11: 11: 11) and turn, leaving rem 10 (11: 11: 12: 13) sts on a holder for collar. 10 (10: 12: 12: 12) sts.
Dec 1 st at neck edge of next 4 rows, then on foll 1 (1: 2: 2: 2) alt rows **and at same time** dec 1 st at raglan edge on 2nd and every foll alt row. 2 sts.
Work 1 row.
Next row (RS): K2tog and fasten off.
With RS facing, rejoin yarn to rem sts, K2tog, K to last 2 sts, K2tog. 32 (33: 35: 36: 37) sts.
Next row (WS): P to last st, K1.
Next row: K to last 2 sts, K2tog.
Last 2 rows set front opening edge st worked as a K st on every row.
Keeping sts correct as set, dec 1 st at raglan edge on 2nd and every foll alt row until 21 (22: 24: 25: 26) sts rem.
Work 1 row, ending with a WS row.
Shape neck
Next row (RS): K10 (11: 11: 12: 13) and slip these sts onto a holder for collar, K to last 2 sts, K2tog.
Complete to match first side, reversing shapings.

SLEEVES

Cast on 49 (51: 53: 55: 57) sts using 3¼mm (US 3) needles and yarn A.
Row 1 (RS): K0 (0: 1: 2: 3), P2 (3: 3: 3: 3), *K5, P3, rep from * to last 7 (0: 1: 2: 3) sts, K5 (0: 1: 2: 3), P2 (0: 0: 0: 0).
Row 2: P0 (0: 1: 2: 3), K2 (3: 3: 3: 3), *P5, K3, rep from * to last 7 (0: 1: 2: 3) sts, P5 (0: 1: 2: 3), K2 (0: 0: 0: 0).
These 2 rows form rib.
Work in rib for a further 8 rows, ending with a WS row.
Change to 4mm (US 6) needles.
Cont in rib, shaping sides by inc 1 st at each end of 5th and every foll 4th (4th: 4th: 6th: 6th) row to 73 (69: 65: 73: 93) sts, then on every foll 6th (6th: 6th: 4th: -) row until there are 77 (81: 85: 89: -) sts, taking inc sts into rib.
Cont straight until sleeve measures 24 (28: 32: 36: 40) cm, ending with a WS row.
Shape raglan
Cast off 5 sts at beg of next 2 rows.
67 (71: 75: 79: 83) sts.
Dec 1 st at each end of next 9 rows, then on every foll alt row until 19 sts rem.
Work 1 row, ending with a WS row.
Left sleeve only
Dec 1 st at each end of next row. 17 sts.
Cast off 3 sts at beg of next row. 14 sts.
Dec 1 st at beg of next row, then cast off 4 sts at beg of foll row. 9 sts.
Rep last 2 rows once more. 4 sts.
Right sleeve only
Cast off 4 sts at beg and dec 1 st at end of next row. 14 sts.
Work 1 row.
Rep last 2 rows twice more. 4 sts.
Both sleeves
Cast off rem 4 sts.

MAKING UP

PRESS as described on the information page.
Join raglan seams using back stitch, or mattress st if preferred.
Collar
With RS facing, using 3¾mm (US 5) needles and yarn A, slip 10 (11: 11: 12: 13) sts on right front holder onto right needle, rejoin yarn and pick up and knit 5 (6: 6: 8: 9) sts up right side of neck, 17 sts from right sleeve, 27 (31: 31: 33: 37) sts from back, 17 sts from left sleeve, 5 (6: 6: 8: 9) sts down left side of neck, then work across 10 (11: 11: 12: 13) sts on left front holder as folls:
K0 (0: 0: 1: 2), P2 (3: 3: 3: 3), K5, P2, K1.
91 (99: 99: 107: 115) sts.
Next row (WS): K3, *P5, K3, rep from * to end.
Next row: K1, P2, *K5, P3, rep from * to last 8 sts, K5, P2, K1.
Rep these 2 rows until collar measures 7 cm from pick-up row, ending with a WS row.
Break off yarn A and join in yarn B.
Change to 3¼mm (US 3) needles.
Next row (RS): K2tog, K to last 2 sts, K2tog.
Beg with a P row, cont in st st until collar measures 7 cm from colour change, ending with a WS row.
Cast off.
See information page for finishing instructions.
Insert zip behind front opening, positioning top of zip just below colour change. Fold last 7 cm of collar (contrast colour section) to inside and slip stitch in position.

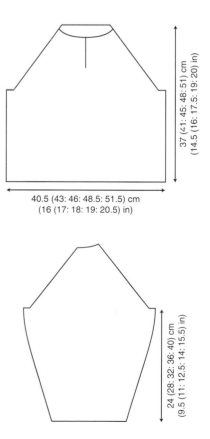

37 (41: 45: 48: 51) cm
(14.5 (16: 17.5: 19: 20) in)

40.5 (43: 46: 48.5: 51.5) cm
(16 (17: 18: 19: 20.5) in)

24 (28: 32: 36: 40) cm
(9.5 (11: 12.5: 14: 15.5) in)

Elliot

YARN

Rowan Rowanspun DK

	6th	7th	8th	9th	10th	size
To fit age	4-5	6-7	8-9	9-10	11-12	years
To fit chest	61	66	71	76	81	cm
	24	26	28	30	32	in
A Mist 738	3	4	4	5	5	x 50gm
B Icy 739	2	3	3	3	4	x 50gm

NEEDLES

1 pair 3¼mm (no 10) (US 3) needles
1 pair 4mm (no 8) (US 6) needles

BUTTONS – 3 x 75315

TENSION

21 sts and 29 rows to 10 cm measured over
stocking stitch using 4mm (US 6) needles.

BACK

Cast on 87 (93: 99: 105: 111) sts using 3¼mm
(US 3) needles and yarn A.
Row 1 (RS): K3, *P3, K3, rep from * to end.
Row 2: P3, *K3, P3, rep from * to end.
These 2 rows form rib.
Work in rib for a further 6 rows, dec 1 st at each
end of last row and ending with a WS row.
85 (91: 97: 103: 109) sts.
Change to 4mm (US 6) needles.
Beg with a K row, cont in st st as folls:
Work 2 rows.
Join in yarn B and now work in striped st st as folls:
Using yarn B, work 10 rows.
Using yarn A, work 10 rows.
These 20 rows form striped st st.
Cont in striped st st until back measures 23 (26:
29: 31: 33) cm, ending with a WS row.
Shape armholes
Keeping stripes correct, cast off 4 sts at beg of
next 2 rows. 77 (83: 89: 95: 101) sts.
Dec 1 st at each end of next 4 rows.
69 (75: 81: 87: 93) sts.
Cont straight until armhole measures 18 (19: 20:
21: 22) cm, ending with a WS row.
Shape shoulders and back neck
Cast off 7 (8: 8: 9: 10) sts at beg of next 2 rows.
55 (59: 65: 69: 73) sts.

Next row (RS): Cast off 7 (8: 8: 9: 10) sts,
K until there are 11 (11: 13: 13: 13) sts on right
needle and turn, leaving rem sts on a holder.
Work each side of neck separately.
Cast off 4 sts at beg of next row.
Cast off rem 7 (7: 9: 9: 9) sts.
With RS facing, rejoin yarn to rem sts, cast off
centre 19 (21: 23: 25: 27) sts, K to end.
Complete to match first side, reversing shapings.

FRONT

Work as given for back until 42 rows less have
been worked than on back to start of shoulder
shaping, ending with a WS row.
Divide for front opening
Keeping stripes correct, cont as folls:
Next row (RS): K36 (39: 42: 45: 48), pick up
loop lying between needles and place loop on
right needle (**note**: this loop does NOT count
as a st), sl next st knitwise and turn, leaving rem
sts on a holder.
37 (40: 43: 46: 49) sts.
Work each side of neck separately.
Next row (WS): P tog first st and the loop,
P to end.
Next row: K to last st, pick up loop lying
between needles and place loop on right needle,
sl last st knitwise.
Last 2 rows form slip st edging at front opening
edge.
Cont as set for a further 5 rows, ending with a
WS row.
Next row (buttonhole row) (RS): K to last
4 sts, yfwd, K2tog, K1, pick up loop lying
between needles and place loop on right needle,
sl last st knitwise.
Work 9 rows.
Rep last 10 rows once more, and then the
buttonhole row again, ending with a RS row.
Shape neck
Next row (WS): P tog first st and the loop,
P9 (10: 11: 12: 13) and slip these 10 (11: 12: 13:
14) sts onto a holder for collar, P to end.
27 (29: 31: 33: 35) sts.
Dec 1 st at neck edge of next 3 rows, then on
foll 3 alt rows.
21 (23: 25: 27: 29) sts.
Work 3 rows, ending with a WS row.
Shape shoulder
Cast off 7 (8: 8: 9: 10) sts at beg of next and foll
alt row.
Work 1 row.
Cast off rem 7 (7: 9: 9: 9) sts.
With RS facing and keeping stripes correct,
rejoin appropriate yarn to rem sts, cast on 5 sts,
K to end. 37 (40: 43: 46: 49) sts.
Next row (WS): P to last st, pick up loop lying
between needles and place loop on right needle
(**note**: this loop does NOT count as a st), sl last
st purlwise.
Next row: K tog tbl first st and the loop, K to
end.
Last 2 rows form slip st edging at front opening
edge.
Cont as set for a further 26 rows, ending with a
RS row.
Shape neck
Next row (WS): P to last 10 (11: 12: 13: 14) sts
and turn, leaving rem sts on a holder.
27 (29: 31: 33: 35) sts.
Complete to match first side, reversing shapings.

SLEEVES (both alike)

Cast on 45 (51: 51: 51: 57) sts using 3¼mm
(US 3) needles and yarn A.

Work in rib as given for back for 8 rows,
inc (dec: –: inc: dec) 1 st at each end of last row
and ending with a WS row. 47 (49: 51: 53: 55) sts.
Change to 4mm (US 6) needles.
Beg with a K row, cont in st st as folls:
Work 2 rows.
Join in yarn B and beg with 10 rows using yarn
B, now work in striped st st as given for back,
shaping sides by inc 1 st at each end of next and
every foll 4th (4th: 4th: 6th: 6th) row to 61 (57:
55: 83: 87) sts, then on every foll 6th (6th: 6th:
8th: 8th) row until there are 75 (79: 83: 87: 91) sts.
Cont straight until sleeve measures 30 (34: 38:
42: 44) cm, ending with a WS row.
Shape top
Cast off 4 sts at beg of next 2 rows.
67 (71: 75: 79: 83) sts.
Dec 1 st at each end of next and foll 4 alt rows.
Work 1 row, ending with a WS row.
Cast off rem 57 (61: 65: 69: 73) sts.

MAKING UP

PRESS as described on the information page.
Join shoulder seams using back stitch, or
mattress st if preferred.
Collar
With RS facing, using 3¼mm (US 10) needles
and yarn A, work across 10 (11: 12: 13: 14) sts on
right front holder as folls: K1, P1, K3, P3, K2 (3:
3: 3: 3), P0 (0: 1: 2: 3), pick up and knit 17 sts up
right side of neck, 25 (29: 33: 31: 35) sts from
back, 17 sts down left side of neck, then work
across 10 (11: 12: 13: 14) sts on left front holder
as folls: P0 (0: 1: 2: 3), K2 (3: 3: 3: 3), P3, K3, P1,
K1. 79 (85: 91: 91: 97) sts.
Next row (RS of collar, WS of body): K2,
*P3, K3, rep from * to last 5 sts, P3, K2.
Next row: K1, P1, *K3, P3, rep from * to last
5 sts, K3, P1, K1.
Rep these 2 rows for 8 cm.
Cast off in rib.
See information page for finishing instructions,
sewing cast-on sts at base of front opening in
place behind left front and setting in sleeves
using the shallow set-in method.

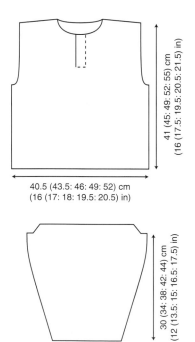

41 (45: 49: 52: 55) cm
(16 (17.5: 19.5: 20.5: 21.5) in)

40.5 (43.5: 46: 49: 52) cm
(16 (17: 18: 19.5: 20.5) in)

30 (34: 38: 42: 44) cm
(12 (13.5: 15: 16.5: 17.5) in)

FREDDIE

YARN

	1st	2nd	3rd	4th	5th	size
	months		years			
To fit age	0-6	6-12	1-2	2-3	3-4	
To fit chest	41	46	51	56	58	cm
	16	18	20	22	23	in
Rowan 4 ply Soft						
A Lime 371	1	1	1	1	1	x 50gm
B Aqua 373	3	3	4	5	6	x 50gm
C Cream 376	1	1	1	1	1	x 50gm

NEEDLES

1 pair 2¾mm (no 12) (US 2) needles
1 pair 3¼mm (no 10) (US 3) needles

TENSION

28 sts and 36 rows to 10 cm measured over
stocking stitch using 3¼mm (US 3) needles.

BACK

Cast on 75 (81: 87: 93: 99) sts using 2¾mm
(US 2) needles and yarn A.
Beg with a K row, work in st st for 8 rows.
Break off yarn A and join in yarn B.
Change to 3¼mm (US 3) needles.
Beg with a K row, cont in st st as folls:
Cont straight until back measures 14 (17: 20: 23:
26) cm, ending with a WS row.

Shape armholes

Cast off 6 sts at beg of next 2 rows.
63 (69: 75: 81: 87) sts.
Cont straight until armhole measures 12 (13: 14:
15: 16) cm, ending with a WS row.

Shape shoulders and back neck

Cast off 5 (6: 6: 7: 8) sts at beg of next 2 rows.
53 (57: 63: 67: 71) sts.
Next row (RS): Cast off 5 (6: 6: 7: 8) sts,
K until there are 9 (9: 11: 11: 11) sts on right
needle and turn, leaving rem sts on a holder.
Work each side of neck separately. Cast off 4 sts
at beg of next row. Cast off rem 5 (5: 7: 7: 7) sts.

1st and 2nd sizes only

With RS facing, slip centre 25 (27: -: -: -) sts
onto a holder, rejoin yarn to rem sts, K to end.

3rd, 4th and 5th sizes only

With RS facing, rejoin yarn to rem sts, cast off
centre - (-: 29: 31: 33) sts, K to end.

All sizes

Complete to match first side, reversing shapings.

FRONT

Work as given for back to beg of armhole
shaping, ending with a WS row.

Shape armholes and place chart

Joining in and breaking off yarn C as necessary,
cont as folls:
Next row (RS): Cast off 6 sts, K until there are
19 (22: 25: 28: 31) sts on right needle, starting
with chart row 1 and using the INTARSIA
method as described on the information page,
work across 25 sts from chart, K to end.
Next row: Cast off 6 sts, P until there are
19 (22: 25: 28: 31) sts on right needle, work
across 25 sts from chart, P to end.
63 (69: 75: 81: 87) sts.
Cont working from chart until chart row 25 has
been completed, ending with a RS row.
Break off yarn C and cont using yarn B only.
Beg with a P row, cont straight until 8 (8: 10: 10:
10) rows less have been worked than on back to
start of shoulder shaping, ending with a WS row.

Shape neck

Next row (RS): K20 (22: 25: 27: 29) and turn,
leaving rem sts on a holder.
Work each side of neck separately.
Dec 1 st at neck edge of next 4 rows, then on
foll 1 (1: 2: 2: 2) alt rows.
15 (17: 19: 21: 23) sts.
Work 1 row, ending with a WS row.

Shape shoulder

Cast off 5 (6: 6: 7: 8) sts at beg of next and foll
alt row.
Work 1 row.
Cast off rem 5 (5: 7: 7: 7) sts.

1st and 2nd sizes only

With RS facing, slip centre 23 (25: -: -: -) sts
onto a holder, rejoin yarn to rem sts, K to end.

3rd, 4th and 5th sizes only

With RS facing, rejoin yarn to rem sts, cast off
centre - (-: 25: 27: 29) sts, K to end.

All sizes

Complete to match first side, reversing shapings.

SLEEVES (both alike)

Cast on 43 (45: 47: 49: 51) sts using 2¾mm
(US 2) needles and yarn A.
Beg with a K row, work in st st for 8 rows.
Break off yarn A and join in yarn B.
Change to 3¼mm (US 3) needles.

Beg with a K row, cont in st st, shaping sides by
inc 1 st at each end of next and every foll 4th
(4th: 4th: 6th: 6th) row until there are 57 (65: 73:
59: 67) sts, then on every foll alt (alt: alt: 4th: 4th)
row until there are 67 (73: 79: 85: 91) sts.
Cont straight until sleeve measures 15 (18: 22:
28: 32) cm, ending with a WS row. Cast off.

MAKING UP

PRESS as described on the information page.
Join right shoulder seam using back stitch, or
mattress st if preferred.

Neckband

With RS facing, using 2¾mm (US 2) needles
and yarn A, pick up and knit 11 (11: 13: 13: 13) sts
down left side of neck, 23 (25: 25: 27: 29) sts
from front, 11 (11: 13: 13: 13) sts up right side of
neck, then 33 (35: 37: 39: 41) sts from back.
78 (82: 88: 92: 96) sts.
Beg with a P row, work in st st for 7 rows.
Cast off **loosely** knitwise.
See information page for finishing instructions,
setting in sleeves using the square set-in method.

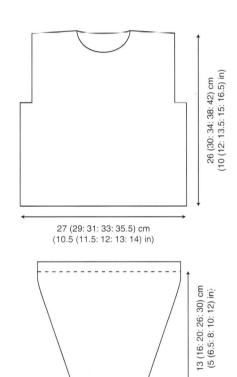

26 (30: 34: 38: 42) cm
(10 (12: 13.5: 15: 16.5) in)

27 (29: 31: 33: 35.5) cm
(10.5 (11.5: 12: 13: 14) in)

13 (16: 20: 26: 30) cm
(5 (6.5: 8: 10: 12) in)

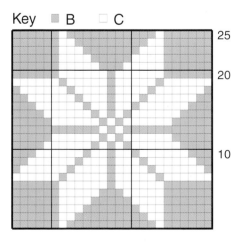

Key ■ B □ C

25
20
10

Jo

YARN

	1st	2nd	3rd	4th	5th	size
To fit age	months		years			
	0-6	6-12	1-2	2-3	3-4	
To fit chest	41	46	51	56	58	cm
	16	18	20	22	23	in
Rowan Denim						
	4	5	7	8	9	x 50gm

	6th	7th	8th	9th	10th	size
To fit age	4-5	6-7	8-9	9-10	11-12	years
To fit chest	61	66	71	76	81	cm
	24	26	28	30	32	in
Rowan Denim						
	11	12	14	16	18	x 50gm

(photographed in Nashville 225)

NEEDLES

1 pair 3¼mm (no 10) (US 3) needles
1 pair 4mm (no 8) (US 6) needles

TENSION

Before washing 20 sts and 28 rows to 10 cm measured over stocking stitch using 4mm (US 6) needles.

Tension note: Denim will shrink in length when washed for the first time. Allowances have been made in this pattern for shrinkage (see size diagram for after washing measurements).

BACK

Cast on 59 (65: 69: 75: 79: 85: 89: 95: 99: 105) sts using 3¼mm (US 3) needles.
Beg with a K row, work in st st for 10 rows.
Change to 4mm (US 6) needles.
Work a further 4 rows in st st.
Beg with a P row, work 4 rows in rev st st.
Beg with a K row, work 6 rows in st st.
Rep last 10 rows once more, then first 4 of these rows again, ending with a WS row.
Starting and ending rows as indicated and repeating the 14 row patt repeat throughout, cont in patt from chart as folls:
Cont straight until back measures 17 (19: 21.5: 25: 29: 32.5: 36: 39.5: 43: 47) cm, ending with a WS row.

Shape armholes

Keeping patt correct, cast off 5 sts at beg of next 2 rows. 49 (55: 59: 65: 69: 75: 79: 85: 89: 95) sts.
Cont straight until armhole measures 13 (15.5: 18: 19: 20.5: 21.5: 23: 24: 25: 26.5) cm, ending with a WS row.

Shape shoulders and back neck

Cast off 4 (5: 6: 6: 7: 8: 8: 9: 9: 10) sts at beg of next 2 rows. 41 (45: 47: 53: 55: 59: 63: 67: 71: 75) sts.
Next row (RS): Cast off 4 (5: 6: 6: 7: 8: 8: 9: 9: 10) sts, patt until there are 9 (10: 9: 11: 11: 11: 12: 13: 14: 14) sts on right needle and turn, leaving rem sts on a holder.
Work each side of neck separately.
Cast off 4 sts at beg of next row.
Cast off rem 5 (6: 5: 7: 7: 7: 8: 9: 10: 10) sts.

1st and 2nd sizes only
With RS facing, slip centre 15 sts onto a holder, rejoin yarn to rem sts, patt to end.

3rd, 4th, 5th, 6th, 7th, 8th, 9th and 10th sizes only
With RS facing, rejoin yarn to rem sts, cast off centre – (-: 17: 19: 19: 21: 23: 23: 25: 27) sts, patt to end.

All sizes
Complete to match first side, reversing shapings.

FRONT

Work as given for back until 12 (12: 12: 12: 14: 14: 14: 16: 16: 16) rows less have been worked than on back to start of shoulder shaping, ending with a WS row.

Shape neck

Next row (RS): Patt 18 (21: 22: 24: 27: 29: 30: 34: 35: 37) sts and turn, leaving rem sts on a holder.
Work each side of neck separately.
Dec 1 st at neck edge of next 2 rows, then on foll 3 (3: 3: 3: 4: 4: 4: 5: 5: 5) alt rows.
13 (16: 17: 19: 21: 23: 24: 27: 28: 30) sts.
Work 3 rows, ending with a WS row.

Shape shoulder

Cast off 4 (5: 6: 6: 7: 8: 8: 9: 9: 10) sts at beg of next and foll alt row.
Work 1 row.
Cast off rem 5 (6: 5: 7: 7: 7: 8: 9: 10: 10) sts.

1st and 2nd sizes only
With RS facing, slip centre 13 sts onto a holder, rejoin yarn to rem sts, patt to end.

3rd, 4th, 5th, 6th, 7th, 8th, 9th and 10th sizes only
With RS facing, rejoin yarn to rem sts, cast off centre – (-: 15: 17: 15: 17: 19: 17: 19: 21) sts, patt to end.

All sizes
Complete to match first side, reversing shapings.

SLEEVES (both alike)

Cast on 33 (35: 37: 39: 41: 43: 45: 47: 49: 51) sts using 3¼mm (US 3) needles.
Beg with a K row, work in st st for 6 rows.
Beg with a P row, work 4 rows in rev st st.
Change to 4mm (US 6) needles.
Starting and ending rows as indicated and repeating the 14 row patt repeat throughout, cont in patt from chart as folls:
Inc 1 st at each end of next and every foll 6th (6th: 4th: 6th: 6th: 6th: 6th: 6th: 6th: 6th) row to 39 (39: 57: 43: 51: 57: 65: 73: 77: 85) sts, then on every foll 4th (4th: alt: 4th: 4th: 4th: 4th: 4th: 4th: 4th) row until there are 45 (53: 61: 65: 69: 73: 77: 81: 85: 89) sts, taking inc sts into patt.
Cont straight until sleeve measures 17 (20.5: 24: 27.5: 31: 35: 38.5: 42: 45.5: 49) cm, ending with a WS row.
Cast off.

MAKING UP

DO NOT PRESS.
Join right shoulder seam using back stitch, or mattress st if preferred.

Neckband
With RS facing and using 3¼mm (US 3) needles, pick up and knit 16 (16: 16: 16: 18: 18: 18: 20: 20: 20) sts down left side of neck, 13 (13: 15: 17: 15: 17: 19: 17: 19: 21) sts from front, 16 (16: 16: 16: 18: 18: 18: 20: 20: 20) sts up right side of neck, then 23 (23: 25: 27: 27: 29: 31: 31: 33: 35) sts from back.
68 (68: 72: 76: 78: 82: 86: 88: 92: 96) sts.
Beg with a P row, work 8 rows in st st.
Cast off **loosely** purlwise.
Machine wash all pieces as described on the ball band before completing garment.
See information page for finishing instructions, setting in sleeves using the square set-in method.

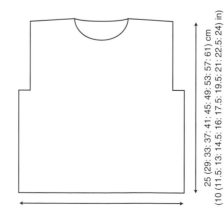

29.5 (32.5: 34.5: 37.5: 39.5: 42.5: 44.5: 47.5: 49.5: 52.5) cm
(11.5 (13: 13.5: 15: 15.5: 16.5: 17.5: 18.5: 19.5: 20.5) in)

25 (29: 33: 37: 41: 45: 49: 53: 57: 61) cm
(10 (11.5: 13: 14.5: 16: 17.5: 19.5: 21: 22.5: 24) in)

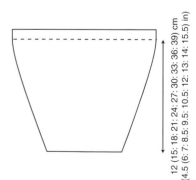

12 (15: 18: 21: 24: 27: 30: 33: 36: 39) cm
(4.5 (6: 7: 8.5: 9.5: 10.5: 12: 13: 14: 15.5) in)

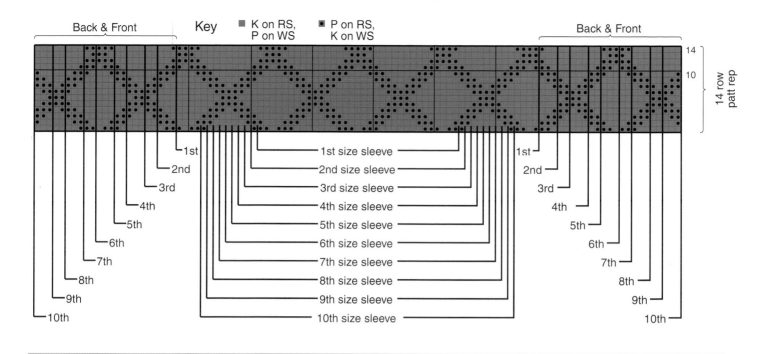

Key   ■ K on RS, P on WS   ▪ P on RS, K on WS

14
10

14 row patt rep

└1st
└2nd
└3rd
└4th
└5th
└6th
└7th
└8th
└9th
└10th

── 1st size sleeve ──
── 2nd size sleeve ──
── 3rd size sleeve ──
── 4th size sleeve ──
── 5th size sleeve ──
── 6th size sleeve ──
── 7th size sleeve ──
── 8th size sleeve ──
── 9th size sleeve ──
── 10th size sleeve ──

1st┘
2nd┘
3rd┘
4th┘
5th┘
6th┘
7th┘
8th┘
9th┘
10th┘

DESIGN NUMBER 16

JESSIE

YARN

Rowan Kid Classic

A Feather	828	2	x	50gm
B Royal	835	1	x	50gm

NEEDLES

1 pair 4mm (no 8) (US 6) needles
1 pair 5mm (no 6) (US 8) needles

BUTTONS – 3 x 75312

TENSION

19 sts and 25 rows to 10 cm measured over stocking stitch using 5mm (US 8) needles.

MEASUREMENTS

Finished cover fits a standard size hot water bottle.

FRONT

Cast on 31 sts using 5mm (US 8) needles and yarn A.
Beg with a K row, work in st st throughout as folls:
Work 1 row.
Inc 1 st at each end of next 6 rows. 43 sts.★★
Work a further 11 rows, ending with a WS row.
Place chart
Join in yarn B and place motif as folls:
Next row (RS): K11, starting with chart row 1 and using the INTARSIA method as described on the information page, work across 21 sts from chart, K to end.
Next row: P11, work across row 2 from chart, P to end.
Cont working from chart until chart row 28 has been completed.
Break off yarn B and cont in st st using yarn A only.
Work a further 18 rows, ending with a WS row.
★★★Shape top
Dec 1 st at each end of next and foll alt row, then on foll 3 rows, ending with a WS row. 33 sts.
Cast off 5 sts at beg of next 2 rows.
Break yarn and leave rem 23 sts on a holder.

LOWER BACK

Work as given for front to ★★.
Work a further 37 rows, ending with a WS row.
Change to 4mm (US 6) needles.
Next row (RS): K2, ★P3, K3, rep from ★ to last 5 sts, P3, K2.
Next row: P2, ★K3, P3, rep from ★ to last 5 sts, K3, P2.
These 2 rows form rib.
Work in rib for a further 6 rows.
Cast off in rib.

UPPER BACK

Cast on 43 sts using 4mm (US 6) needles and yarn A.
Work in rib as given for lower back for 4 rows.
Row 5 (buttonhole row) (RS): Rib 8, ★P2tog, yrn, rib 10, rep from ★ once more P2tog, yrn, rib 9.

Work in rib for a further 3 rows, ending with a WS row.
Change to 5mm (US 8) needles.
Beg with a K row, work in st st throughout as folls:
Work 14 rows, ending with a WS row.
Complete as given for front from ★★★.

MAKING UP

PRESS as described on the information page.
Top border
With RS facing, using 4mm (US 6) needles and yarn A, K 23 sts of front, then K 23 sts of upper back. 46 sts.
Row 1 (WS): P2, ★K2, P2, rep from ★ to end.
Row 2: K2, ★P2, K2, rep from ★ to end.
Rep these 2 rows for 8 cm.
Change to 5mm (US 8) needles and work a further 8 cm in rib.
Cast off in rib.
Lay upper back over lower back so that ribbed sections meet and sew together at side edges.
Sew front to back sections along side and base seam.
Join neck seam, reversing seam for last 10 cm of top border for turn-back.
Attach buttons to correspond with buttonholes.

Key ☐ A ■ B

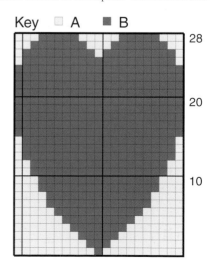

28
20
10

Rose

YARN

	1st	2nd	3rd	4th	5th	size
To fit age	months			years		
	0-6	6-12	1-2	2-3	3-4	
To fit chest	41	46	51	56	58	cm
	16	18	20	22	23	in
Rowan Wool Cotton						
A Rich 911	1	1	1	1	1	x 50gm
B Clear 941	2	3	3	4	4	x 50gm

	6th	7th	8th	9th	10th	size
To fit age	4-5	6-7	8-9	9-10	11-12	years
To fit chest	61	66	71	76	81	cm
	24	26	28	30	32	in
Rowan Wool Cotton						
A Rich 911	2	2	2	2	2	x 50gm
B Clear 941	5	6	7	8	9	x 50gm

NEEDLES

1 pair 3¼mm (no 10) (US 3) needles
1 pair 4mm (no 8) (US 6) needles

BUTTONS – 4 (4: 4: 4: 4: 5: 5: 5: 5: 5) x 75337

TENSION

22 sts and 30 rows to 10 cm measured over stocking stitch using 4mm (US 6) needles.

BACK

Cast on 49 (55: 61: 67: 73: 79: 85: 91: 97: 103) sts using 3¼mm (US 3) needles and yarn A.
Row 1 (RS): K1, *P1, K1, rep from * to end.
Row 2: As row 1.
These 2 rows form moss st.
Work in moss st for a further 5 rows, ending with a RS row.
Row 8 (WS): Purl.
Break off yarn A and join in yarn B.
Change to 4mm (US 6) needles.
Beg with a K row, cont in st st as folls:
Cont straight until back measures 10 (12: 14: 16: 19: 22: 25: 28: 31: 34) cm, ending with a WS row.
Shape armholes
Cast off 3 (3: 3: 3: 3: 4: 4: 4: 4: 4) sts at beg of next 2 rows. 43 (49: 55: 61: 67: 71: 77: 83: 89: 95) sts.
Dec 1 st at each end of next 3 (3: 3: 3: 3: 4: 4: 4: 4: 4) rows. 37 (43: 49: 55: 61: 63: 69: 75: 81: 87) sts.

Cont straight until armhole measures 11 (12: 13: 14: 15: 16: 17: 18: 19: 20) cm, ending with a WS row.
Shape shoulders and back neck
Cast off 3 (4: 4: 5: 6: 6: 7: 8: 8: 9) sts at beg of next 2 rows. 31 (35: 41: 45: 49: 51: 55: 59: 65: 69) sts.
Next row (RS): Cast off 3 (4: 4: 5: 6: 6: 7: 8: 8: 9) sts, K until there are 6 (7: 9: 10: 10: 10: 11: 11: 13: 14) sts on right needle and turn, leaving rem sts on a holder.
Work each side of neck separately.
Cast off 4 sts at beg of next row.
Cast off rem 2 (3: 5: 6: 6: 6: 7: 7: 9: 10) sts.
With RS facing, rejoin yarn to rem sts, cast off centre 13 (13: 15: 15: 17: 19: 19: 21: 23: 23) sts, K to end.
Complete to match first side, reversing shapings.

LEFT FRONT

Cast on 29 (33: 35: 39: 41: 45: 47: 51: 53: 57) sts using 3¼mm (US 3) needles and yarn A.
Work in moss st as for back for 7 rows, ending with a RS row.
Row 8 (WS): Moss st 6 sts and slip these sts onto a holder for button band, M1, P to last 1 (0: 1: 0: 1: 0: 1: 0: 1: 0) st, (inc in last st) 1 (0: 1: 0: 1: 0: 1: 0: 1: 0) times.
25 (28: 31: 34: 37: 40: 43: 46: 49: 52) sts.
Break off yarn A and join in yarn B.
Change to 4mm (US 6) needles.
Beg with a K row, cont in st st as folls:
Cont straight until left front matches back to beg of armhole shaping, ending with a WS row.
Shape armhole
Cast off 3 (3: 3: 3: 3: 4: 4: 4: 4: 4) sts at beg of next row. 22 (25: 28: 31: 34: 36: 39: 42: 45: 48) sts.
Work 1 row.
Shape front slope
Dec 1 st at armhole edge of next 3 (3: 3: 3: 3: 4: 4: 4: 4: 4) rows **and at same time** dec 1 st at front slope edge of next and foll alt row.
17 (20: 23: 26: 29: 30: 33: 36: 39: 42) sts.
Dec 1 st at front slope edge **only** on 2nd (2nd: 2nd: 2nd: 2nd: next: next: next: next: next) and foll 6 (4: 5: 3: 4: 4: 3: 3: 4: 2) alt rows, then on every foll 4th row until 8 (11: 13: 16: 18: 18: 21: 23: 25: 28) sts rem.
Cont straight until left front matches back to start of shoulder shaping, ending with a WS row.
Shape shoulder
Cast off 3 (4: 4: 5: 6: 6: 7: 8: 8: 9) sts at beg of next and foll alt row.
Work 1 row.
Cast off rem 2 (3: 5: 6: 6: 6: 7: 7: 9: 10) sts.

RIGHT FRONT

Cast on 29 (33: 35: 39: 41: 45: 47: 51: 53: 57) sts using 3¼mm (US 3) needles and yarn A.

Work in moss st as for back for 4 rows, ending with a WS row.
Row 5 (buttonhole row) (RS): Moss st 2 sts, work 2 tog, yrn (to make a buttonhole), moss st to end.
Work in moss st for a further 2 rows, ending with a RS row.
Row 8 (WS): (Inc in first st) 1 (0: 1: 0: 1: 0: 1: 0: 1: 0) times, P to last 6 sts, M1 and turn, leaving last 6 sts on a holder for buttonhole band.
25 (28: 31: 34: 37: 40: 43: 46: 49: 52) sts.
Break off yarn A and join in yarn B.
Change to 4mm (US 6) needles.
Beg with a K row, cont in st st and complete to match first side, reversing shapings.

SLEEVES (both alike)

Cast on 33 (35: 37: 39: 41: 43: 45: 47: 49: 51) sts using 3¼mm (US 3) needles and yarn A.
Work in moss st as for back for 7 rows, ending with a RS row.
Row 8 (WS): Purl.
Break off yarn A and join in yarn B.
Change to 4mm (US 6) needles.
Beg with a K row, cont in st st, shaping sides by inc 1 st at each end of 3rd and every foll 4th (4th: 6th: 6th: 6th: 6th: 6th: 8th: 8th: 8th) row to 43 (51: 41: 51: 57: 61: 69: 55: 57: 61) sts, then on every foll alt (alt: 4th: 4th: 4th: 4th: 4th: 6th: 6th: 6th) row until there are 49 (53: 57: 61: 65: 69: 73: 77: 81: 85) sts.
Cont straight until sleeve measures 13 (16: 20: 24: 27: 30: 33: 39: 42: 45) cm, ending with a WS row.
Shape top
Cast off 3 (3: 3: 3: 3: 4: 4: 4: 4: 4) sts at beg of next 2 rows. 43 (47: 51: 55: 59: 61: 65: 69: 73: 77) sts.
Dec 1 st at each end of next and foll 2 (2: 2: 2: 2: 3: 3: 3: 3: 3) alt rows.
Work 1 row, ending with a WS row.
Cast off rem 37 (41: 45: 49: 53: 53: 57: 61: 65: 69) sts.

MAKING UP

PRESS as described on the information page.
Join shoulder seams using back stitch, or mattress st if preferred.
Button band
Slip 6 sts left on left front holder onto 3¼mm (US 3) needles and rejoin yarn A with RS facing.
Cont in moss st as set until band, when slightly stretched, fits up left front opening edge, up front slope and across to centre back neck.
Cast off.
Slip stitch band in place.
Mark positions for 4 (4: 4: 4: 4: 5: 5: 5: 5: 5) buttons on this band – first to come level with

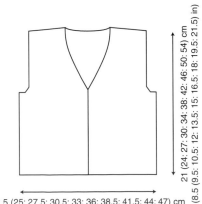

22.5 (25: 27.5: 30.5: 33: 36: 38.5: 41.5: 44: 47) cm
(9 (10: 11: 12: 13: 14: 15: 16.5: 17.5: 18.5) in)

21 (24: 27: 30: 34: 38: 42: 46: 50: 54) cm
(8.5 (9.5: 10.5: 12: 13.5: 15: 16.5: 18: 19.5: 21.5) in)

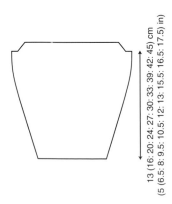

13 (16: 20: 24: 27: 30: 33: 39: 42: 45) cm
(5 (6.5: 8: 9.5: 10.5: 12: 13: 15.5: 16.5: 17.5) in)

buttonhole already worked in right front, last to come just below front slope shaping and rem buttons evenly spaced between.
Buttonhole band
Work to match button band, rejoining yarn A

with WS facing and with the addition of a further 3 (3: 3: 3: 3: 4: 4: 4: 4: 4) buttonholes worked to correspond with positions marked for buttons as folls:
Buttonhole row (RS): Moss st 2 sts, work 2 tog, yrn (to make a buttonhole), moss st 2 sts.
Slip stitch band in place, joining cast-off ends at centre back neck.
See information page for finishing instructions, setting in sleeves using the shallow set-in method.

JAKE

YARN

	1st	2nd	3rd	4th–5th	size
To fit age	months		years		
	0-6	6-12	1-2	2-4	
To fit chest					
	41	46	51	56-58	cm
	16	18	20	22-23	in
Rowan All Seasons Cotton					
	3	3	4	5	x 50gm

5th-6th	7th	8th	9th	10th	size
To fit age					
3-5	6-7	8-9	9-10	11-12	years
To fit chest					
58-61	66	71	76	81	cm
23-24	26	28	30	32	in
Rowan All Seasons Cotton					
6	8	8	10	12	x 50gm

(photographed in Silver 173)

NEEDLES
1 pair 4mm (no 8) (US 6) needles
1 pair 4½mm (no 7) (US 7) needles
1 pair 5mm (no 6) (US 8) needles

TENSION
17 sts and 24 rows to 10 cm measured over stocking stitch using 5mm (US 8) needles.

BACK
Cast on 42 (49: 56: 63: 70: 77: 84: 91: 98) sts using 4½mm (US 7) needles.
Row 1 (RS): K6 (7: 8: 9: 10: 11: 12: 13: 14), *P6 (7: 8: 9: 10: 11: 12: 13: 14), K6 (7: 8: 9: 10: 11: 12: 13: 14), rep from * to end.
Row 2: P6 (7: 8: 9: 10: 11: 12: 13: 14), *K6 (7: 8: 9: 10: 11: 12: 13: 14), P6 (7: 8: 9: 10: 11: 12: 13: 14), rep from * to end.

Rep last 2 rows 3 (4: 5: 5: 6: 7: 7: 8: 9) times more.
Change to 5mm (US 8) needles.
Next row (RS): P6 (7: 8: 9: 10: 11: 12: 13: 14), *K6 (7: 8: 9: 10: 11: 12: 13: 14), P6 (7: 8: 9: 10: 11: 12: 13: 14), rep from * to end.
Next row: K6 (7: 8: 9: 10: 11: 12: 13: 14), *P6 (7: 8: 9: 10: 11: 12: 13: 14), K6 (7: 8: 9: 10: 11: 12: 13: 14), rep from * to end.
Rep last 2 rows 3 (4: 5: 5: 6: 7: 7: 8: 9) times more.
Last 16 (20: 24: 24: 28: 32: 32: 36: 40) rows form block patt.
Cont in patt until 4 bands of blocks have been completed, ending with a WS row. Work should measure 13 (16: 20: 20: 23: 27: 27: 30: 33) cm.
Shape armholes
Keeping patt correct, cast off 4 (4: 4: 4: 5: 5: 5: 5: 5) sts at beg of next 2 rows.
34 (41: 48: 55: 60: 67: 74: 81: 88) sts.
Cont in patt until 7 bands of blocks have been completed, ending with a WS row. Armhole should measure 10 (13: 15: 15: 18: 20: 20: 23: 25) cm.
Shape shoulders and back neck
Cast off 2 (3: 4: 5: 6: 7: 8: 9: 10) sts at beg of next 2 rows. 30 (35: 40: 45: 48: 53: 58: 63: 68) sts.
Next row (RS): Cast off 2 (3: 4: 5: 6: 7: 8: 9: 10) sts, patt until there are 6 (7: 9: 10: 10: 11: 12: 13: 14) sts on right needle and turn, leaving rem sts on a holder.
Work each side of neck separately.
Cast off 3 (3: 4: 4: 4: 4: 4: 4: 4) sts at beg of next row.
Cast off rem 3 (4: 5: 6: 6: 7: 8: 9: 10) sts.
With RS facing, rejoin yarn to rem sts, cast off centre 14 (15: 14: 15: 16: 17: 18: 19: 20) sts, patt to end.
Complete to match first side, reversing shapings.

FRONT
Work as given for back until 10 rows less have been worked than on back to start of shoulder shaping, ending with a WS row.
Shape neck
Next row (RS): Patt 13 (16: 19: 22: 24: 27: 30: 33: 36) sts and turn, leaving rem sts on a holder.
Work each side of neck separately.
Dec 1 st at neck edge of next 4 rows, then on foll 2 alt rows. 7 (10: 13: 16: 18: 21: 24: 27: 30) sts.

Work 1 row, ending with a WS row.
Shape shoulder
Cast off 2 (3: 4: 5: 6: 7: 8: 9: 10) sts at beg of next and foll alt row.
Work 1 row.
Cast off rem 3 (4: 5: 6: 6: 7: 8: 9: 10) sts.
With RS facing, rejoin yarn to rem sts, cast off centre 8 (9: 10: 11: 12: 13: 14: 15: 16) sts, patt to end.
Complete to match first side, reversing shapings.

SLEEVES (both alike)
Cast on 28 (31: 34: 37: 40: 43: 44: 45: 46) sts using 4½mm (US 7) needles.
Beg with a K row, cont in st st as folls:
Work 6 (6: 8: 8: 8: 10: 10: 10: 10) rows, ending with a WS row.
Change to 5mm (US 8) needles.
Cont in st st, shaping sides by inc 1 st at each end of next and every foll 10th (6th: 4th: 8th: 6th: 4th: 4th: 4th: 4th) row to 32 (39: 40: 51: 54: 57: 48: 59: 72) sts, then on every foll 12th (8th: 6th: –: 8th: 6th: 6th: 6th: 6th) row until there are 34 (43: 50: –: 60: 69: 70: 77: 84) sts **and at same time** when sleeve measures 10 (12: 16: 18: 20: 21: 25: 28: 28) cm, work centre 6 (7: 8: 9: 10: 11: 12: 13: 14) sts in rev st st for 8 (10: 12: 12: 14: 16: 16: 18: 20) rows to form block.
Cont straight until sleeve measures 16 (20: 24: 28: 33: 36: 40: 44: 46) cm, ending with a WS row.
Cast off.

MAKING UP
PRESS as described on the information page.
Join right shoulder seam using back stitch, or mattress st if preferred.
Neckband
With RS facing and using 4mm (US 6) needles, pick up and knit 14 sts down left side of neck, 8 (9: 10: 11: 12: 13: 14: 15: 16) sts from front, 14 sts up right side of neck, then 20 (21: 22: 23: 24: 25: 26: 27: 28) sts from back. 56 (58: 60: 62: 64: 66: 68: 70: 72) sts.
Beg with a P row, work in st st for 6 rows.
Cast off **loosely** purlwise.
See information page for finishing instructions, setting in sleeves using the square set-in method.

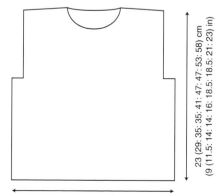

24.5 (29: 33: 37: 41: 45.5: 49.5: 53.5: 57.5) cm
(9.5 (11.5: 13: 14.5: 16: 18: 19.5: 21: 22.5) in)

23 (29: 35: 35: 41: 47: 47: 53: 58) cm
(9 (11.5: 14: 14: 16: 18.5: 18.5: 21: 23) in)

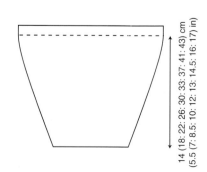

14 (18: 22: 26: 30: 33: 37: 41: 43) cm
(5.5 (7: 8.5: 10: 12: 13: 14.5: 16: 17) in)

ELLIE

YARN

	6th	7th	8th	9th	10th size
To fit age	4-5	6-7	8-9	9-10	11-12 years
To fit chest	61	66	71	76	81 cm
	24	26	28	30	32 in
Rowan Polar	5	6	7	8	9 x100gm

(photographed in Stormy 647)

NEEDLES

1 pair 7mm (no 2) (US 10½) needles
1 pair 8mm (no 0) (US 11) needles

BUTTONS – 4 x 75336, and 1 x 75315

TENSION

12 sts and 21 rows to 10 cm measured over moss stitch using 8mm (US 11) needles.

BACK

Cast on 47 (51: 55: 59: 63) sts using 7mm (US 10½) needles.
Row 1 (RS): K1, *P1, K1, rep from * to end.
Row 2: As row 1.
These 2 rows form moss st.
Work a further 4 rows in moss st.
Change to 8mm (US 11) needles.
Cont straight in moss st until back measures 24 (27: 30: 32: 34) cm, ending with a WS row.
Shape raglan armholes
Keeping moss st correct, cast off 4 sts at beg of next 2 rows. 39 (43: 47: 51: 55) sts.
Dec 1 st at each end of next 1 (3: 3: 5: 5) rows, then on every foll alt row until 9 (9: 11: 11: 13) sts rem, then on foll row, ending with a WS row.
Cast off rem 7 (7: 9: 9: 11) sts.

POCKET LININGS (make 2)

Cast on 11 (13: 13: 15: 15) sts using 8mm (US 11) needles.
Work in moss st as given for back for 22 (24: 24: 26: 26) rows.
Break yarn and leave sts on a holder.

LEFT FRONT

Cast on 27 (29: 31: 33: 35) sts using 7mm (US 10½) needles.
Work in moss st as given for back for 6 rows.

Change to 8mm (US 11) needles.
Cont straight in moss st until left front measures 14 (16: 18: 19: 20) cm, ending with a WS row.
Place pocket
Next row (RS): Moss st 6 sts, slip next 11 (13: 13: 15: 15) sts onto a holder and, in their place, moss st across 11 (13: 13: 15: 15) sts of first pocket lining, moss st 10 (10: 12: 12: 14) sts.
Cont straight in moss st until left front matches back to beg of raglan armhole shaping, ending with a WS row.
Shape raglan armhole
Keeping moss st correct, cast off 4 sts at beg of next row. 23 (25: 27: 29: 31) sts.
Work 1 row.
Dec 1 st at raglan edge of next 1 (3: 3: 5: 5) rows, then on every foll alt row until 14 (14: 15: 16: 17) sts rem, ending with a RS row.
Shape neck
Cast off 6 (6: 7: 6: 7) sts at beg of next row. 8 (8: 8: 10: 10) sts.
Dec 1 st at neck edge of next 3 rows, then on foll 1 (1: 1: 2: 2) alt rows and at same time dec 1 st at raglan edge of next and every foll alt row. 1 st.
Work 1 row, ending with a WS row.
Fasten off.
Mark positions for 4 buttons along left front opening edge – first to come 12 (14: 16: 17: 18) cm up from cast-on edge, last to come 1.5 cm below neck shaping and rem 2 buttons evenly spaced between.

RIGHT FRONT

Cast on 27 (29: 31: 33: 35) sts using 7mm (US 10½) needles.
Work in moss st as given for back for 6 rows.
Change to 8mm (US 11) needles.
Cont straight in moss st until right front measures 12 (14: 16: 17: 18) cm, ending with a WS row.
Next row (buttonhole row) (RS): Moss st 3 sts, work 2 tog, yrn (to make a buttonhole) moss st to end.
Making a further 3 buttonholes in this way to correspond with positions marked on left front for buttons and noting that no further reference will be made to buttonholes, cont straight until right front measures 14 (16: 18: 19: 20) cm, ending with a WS row.
Place pocket
Next row (RS): Moss st 10 (10: 12: 12: 14) sts, slip next 11 (13: 13: 15: 15) sts onto a holder and, in their place, moss st across 11 (13: 13: 15: 15) sts of second pocket lining, moss st 6 sts.
Complete to match left front, reversing shapings.

SLEEVES

Cast on 31 (33: 33: 35: 35) sts using 8mm (US 11) needles.
Work in moss st as given for back, shaping sides by inc 1 st at each end of 7th (9th: 9th: 11th: 11th) and every foll 8th (8th: 8th: 10th: 10th) row to 41 (37: 39: 43: 47) sts, then on every foll – (10th: 10th: 12th: 12th) row until there are – (43: 45: 47: 49) sts.
Cont straight until sleeve measures 22 (26: 30: 34: 38) cm, ending with a WS row.
Shape raglan
Cast off 4 sts at beg of next 2 rows.
33 (35: 37: 39: 41) sts.
Dec 1 st at each end of next and every foll 4th row to 23 (25: 27: 29: 31) sts, then on every foll alt row until 17 sts rem.
Work 1 row, ending with a WS row.

Left sleeve only
Dec 1 st at each end of next row. 15 sts.
Cast off 3 sts at beg of next row. 12 sts.
Dec 1 st at beg of next row, then cast off 3 sts at beg of foll row. 8 sts.
Rep last 2 rows once more. 4 sts.
Right sleeve only
Cast off 4 sts at beg and dec 1 st at end of next row. 12 sts.
Work 1 row.
Cast off 3 sts at beg and dec 1 st at end of next row. 8 sts.
Work 1 row.
Rep last 2 rows once more. 4 sts.
Both sleeves
Cast off rem 4 sts.

MAKING UP

PRESS as described on the information page.
Join raglan seams using back stitch, or mattress st if preferred.
Collar
Cast on 47 (49: 51: 53: 55) sts using 7mm (US 10½) needles.
Work in moss st as given for back for 8 cm.
Cast off in moss st.
Starting and ending 5 sts in from front opening edges, sew cast-on edge of collar to neck edge.
Pocket tops (both alike)
Slip 11 (13: 13: 15: 15) pocket sts left on holder onto 7mm (US 10½) needles and rejoin yarn with RS facing.
Work in moss st as for back for 2 rows.
Cast off in moss st.
See information page for finishing instructions.
Sew on larger buttons to correspond with buttonholes. Sew smaller button at front opening edge of collar and either make a buttonloop to correspond or enlarge a st to form a buttonhole.

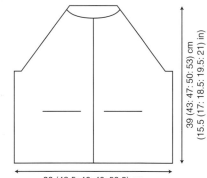

39 (42.5: 46: 49: 52.5) cm
(15.5 (16.5: 18: 19.5: 20.5) in)

39 (43: 47: 50: 53) cm
(15.5 (17: 18.5: 19.5: 21) in)

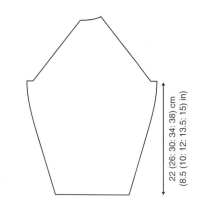

22 (26: 30: 34: 38) cm
(8.5 (10: 12: 13.5: 15) in)

Lou

YARN

Rowan Big Wool

	6th	7th	8th	9th	10th	size
To fit age	4-5	6-7	8-9	9-10	11-12	years
To fit chest	61	66	71	76	81	cm
	24	26	28	30	32	in
	4	4	5	5	6	x 100gm

(photographed in Merry Berry 006)

NEEDLES

1 pair 15mm (US 19) needles

BUTTONS - 3 x 75336

TENSION

7½ sts and 10 rows to 10 cm measured over stocking stitch using 15mm (US 19) needles.

BACK and FRONTS

(worked in one piece to armholes)
Cast on 61 (65: 69: 73: 77) sts using 15mm (US 19) needles.
Work in garter st for 5 rows, ending with **wrong** side row.
Next row (RS): Knit.
Next row: K4, P to last 4 sts, K4.
These 2 rows set the sts – 4 st garter st border at each end of row and st st between.
Keeping sts correct, cont as folls:
Work a further 0 (0: 0: 0: 2) rows.
Place markers 17 (18: 19: 20: 21) sts in from ends of last row, leaving 27 (29: 31: 33: 35) sts between markers.
Next row (dec) (RS): *K to within 3 sts of marker, K2tog, K2 (marker sits between these sts), K2tog tbl, rep from * once more, K to end.
57 (61: 65: 69: 73) sts.
Work 1 (3: 3: 3: 3) rows.
Next row (dec) (RS): *K to within 3 sts of marker, K2tog, K2, K2tog tbl, rep from * once more, K to end.
53 (57: 61: 65: 69) sts.
Work 3 (3: 5: 5: 5) rows.
Next row (inc) (RS): *K to within 1 st of marker, M1, K2 (marker sits between these sts), M1, rep from * once more, K to end.
57 (61: 65: 69: 73) sts.

Work 3 rows.
Next row (inc) (RS): *K to within 1 st of marker, M1, K2, M1, rep from * once more, K to end. 61 (65: 69: 73: 77) sts.
Work a further 1 (1: 1: 3: 3) rows, ending with a WS row. Work should measure approx 19 (21: 23: 25: 27) cm.

Divide for raglan armholes

Next row (RS): K15 (16: 17: 18: 19) and slip these sts onto a holder for right front, cast off next 4 sts, K until there are 23 (25: 27: 29: 31) sts on right needle after cast off and slip these sts onto another holder for back, cast off next 4 sts, K to end.
Work on this last set of 15 (16: 17: 18: 19) sts for left front as folls:
Work 1 row.
Next row (RS): K2tog, K to last 4 sts and turn, leaving last 4 sts on a holder for left collar.
10 (11: 12: 13: 14) sts.
Dec 1 (0: 1: 0: 1) st at raglan armhole edge of next row. 9 (11: 11: 13: 13) sts.
Dec 1 st at each end of next and every foll alt row until 1 st rem.
Next row (WS): P1 and fasten off.

Shape back

With WS facing, rejoin yarn to 23 (25: 27: 29: 31) sts from back and work 1 row.
Dec 1 st at each end of next 3 (1: 3: 1: 3) rows, then on foll 4 (6: 5: 7: 6) alt rows, then on foll row, ending with a WS row.
Cast off rem 7 (9: 9: 11: 11) sts.

Shape right front

With WS facing, rejoin yarn to 15 (16: 17: 18: 19) sts from right front and work 1 row.
Next row (RS): K4 and slip these 4 sts onto a holder for right collar, K to last 2 sts, K2tog.
10 (11: 12: 13: 14) sts.
Dec 1 (0: 1: 0: 1) st at raglan armhole edge of next row. 9 (11: 11: 13: 13) sts.
Dec 1 st at each end of next and every foll alt row until 1 st rem.
Next row (WS): P1 and fasten off.

SLEEVES

Cast on 15 (17: 17: 19: 19) sts using 15mm (US 19) needles.
Work in garter st for 5 rows, ending with **wrong** side row.
Beg with a K row, cont in st st as folls:

Inc 1 st at each end of next and every foll 4th (6th: 6th: 8th: 8th) row until there are 25 (25: 27: 27: 29) sts.
Cont straight until sleeve measures 28 (32: 36: 40: 44) cm, ending with a WS row.

Shape raglan

Cast off 2 sts at beg of next 2 rows.
21 (21: 23: 23: 25) sts.
Dec 1 st at each end of next 3 (1: 3: 1: 3) rows, then on every foll alt row until 9 sts rem, ending with a RS row.
Work 1 row, ending with a WS row.

Left sleeve only

Dec 1 st at each of next row. 7 sts.
Cast off 3 sts at beg and dec 1 st at end of next row.

Right sleeve only

Cast off 4 sts at beg and dec 1 st at end of next row. 4 sts.
Dec 1 st at end of next row.

Both sleeves

Cast off rem 3 sts.

MAKING UP

PRESS as described on the information page.
Join raglan seams using back stitch, or mattress st if preferred. Join side and sleeve seams.

Left collar

Slip 4 sts from left collar holder onto 15mm (US 19) needles and rejoin yarn with RS facing. Working in garter st throughout, cont as folls:
Work 1 row.
Inc 1 st at inner attached end (beg) of next and every foll alt row until there are 9 (11: 11: 13: 13) sts.
Cont straight until collar, unstretched, fits up left front slope, across top of left sleeve and across to centre back neck.
Cast off.

Right collar

Work to match left collar, rejoining yarn with WS facing and reversing shaping.
Join centre back seam of collar, then slip stitch collar in position. Sew 3 buttons to left front – first to come 5 cm up from lower edge, last to come 1 cm below start of front slope shaping, and rem button midway between. To fasten buttons, push them through knitting of right front, enlarging a stitch if required.
See information page for finishing instructions.

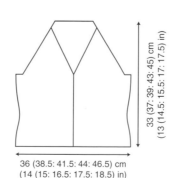

36 (38.5: 41.5: 44: 46.5) cm
(14 (15: 16.5: 17.5: 18.5) in)

33 (37: 39: 43: 45) cm
(13 (14.5: 15.5: 17: 17.5) in)

28 (32: 36: 40: 44) cm
(11 (12.5: 14: 15.5: 17.5) in)

Trixi

YARN
Rowan Wool Cotton

		3rd	4th	5th	size
To fit age		1-2	2-3	3-4	years
To fit chest		51	56	58	cm
		20	22	23	in
A Citron	901	3	4	4	x 50gm
B Aqua	949	1	1	1	x 50gm

		7th	8th	9th	10th	size
To fit age		6-7	8-9	9-10	11-12	years
To fit chest		66	71	76	81	cm
		26	28	30	32	in
A Citron	901	5	6	7	7	x 50gm
B Aqua	949	1	1	1	1	x 50gm

NEEDLES
1 pair 3 mm (no 11) (US 2/3) needles
1 pair 3¼mm (no 10) (US 3) needles
1 pair 4mm (no 8) (US 6) needles
Cable needle

ZIP – open-ended zip to fit

TENSION
22 sts and 30 rows to 10 cm measured over stocking stitch using 4mm (US 6) needles.

BACK
Cast on 58 (64: 70: 76: 82: 88: 94) sts using 3¼mm (US 3) needles and yarn A.
Row 1 (RS): K0 (0: 0: 1: 0: 0: 0), P2 (1: 0: 2: 2: 1: 0), *K2, P2, rep from * to last 0 (3: 2: 1: 0: 3: 2) sts, K0 (2: 2: 1: 0: 2: 2), P0 (1: 0: 0: 0: 1: 0).
Row 2: P0 (0: 0: 1: 0: 0: 0), K2 (1: 0: 2: 2: 1: 0), *P2, K2, rep from * to last 0 (3: 2: 1: 0: 3: 2) sts, P0 (2: 2: 1: 0: 2: 2), K0 (1: 0: 0: 0: 1: 0).
These 2 rows form rib.
Work in rib for a further 14 (14: 14: 6: 8: 10: 12) rows, ending with a WS row.
7th, 8th, 9th and 10th sizes only
Dec 1 st at each end of next and every foll 4th row until - (-: -: 70: 78: 84: 90) sts rem.
Work a further - (-: -: 1: 3: 3: 1) rows.
All sizes
16 (16: 16: 18: 18: 20: 20) rows of rib have now been completed.

Change to 4mm (US 6) needles.
Beg with a K row, cont in st st as folls:
7th, 8th, 9th and 10th sizes only
Work - (-: -: 2: 0: 0: 2) rows, ending with a WS row.
Next row (RS): K2, K2tog, K to last 4 sts, K2tog tbl, K2.
Working all decreases as set by last row, dec 1 st at each end of every foll 4th row until - (-: -: 66: 72: 76: 82) sts rem.
Work - (-: -: 5: 7: 7: 7) rows, ending with a WS row.
Next row (RS): K2, M1, K to last 2 sts, M1, K2.
Working all increases as set by last row, inc 1 st at each end of every foll - (-: -: 6th: 8th: 6th: 8th) row until there are - (-: -: 76: 82: 88: 94) sts.
All sizes
Cont straight until back measures 12 (15: 18: 21: 24: 27: 30) cm, ending with a WS row.
Shape armholes
Cast off 2 (2: 3: 3: 4: 4: 4) sts at beg of next 2 rows.
54 (60: 64: 70: 74: 80: 86) sts.
Dec 1 st at each end of next 1 (1: 1: 3: 3: 3: 3) rows, then on foll 1 (2: 2: 1: 1: 2: 3) alt rows.
50 (54: 58: 62: 66: 70: 74) sts.
Cont straight until armhole measures 12 (13: 14: 15: 16: 17: 18) cm, ending with a WS row.
Shape shoulders and back neck
Cast off 5 (5: 6: 6: 7: 7: 8) sts at beg of next 2 rows.
40 (44: 46: 50: 52: 56: 58) sts.
Next row (RS): Cast off 5 (5: 6: 6: 7: 7: 8) sts, K until there are 8 (10: 10: 11: 11: 12: 12) sts on right needle and turn, leaving rem sts on a holder.
Work each side of neck separately.
Cast off 4 sts at beg of next row.
Cast off rem 4 (6: 6: 7: 7: 8: 8) sts.
With RS facing, rejoin yarn to rem sts, cast off centre 14 (14: 14: 16: 16: 18: 18) sts, K to end.
Complete to match first side, reversing shapings.

LEFT FRONT
Cast on 35 (38: 41: 44: 47: 50: 53) sts using 3¼mm (US 3) needles and yarn A.
Row 1 (RS): K0 (0: 0: 1: 0: 0: 0), P2 (1: 0: 2: 2: 1: 0), *K2, P2, rep from * to last 13 sts, (K4, P2) twice, K1.
Row 2: K1, (K2, P4) twice, K2, *P2, K2, rep from * to last 0 (3: 2: 1: 0: 3: 2) sts, P0 (2: 2: 1: 0: 2: 2), K0 (1: 0: 0: 0: 0: 1: 0).
These 2 rows form rib.
Work in rib for a further 14 (14: 14: 6: 8: 10: 12) rows, ending with a WS row.
7th, 8th, 9th and 10th sizes only
Dec 1 st at beg of next and every foll 4th row until - (-: -: 41: 45: 48: 51) sts rem.
Work a further - (-: -: 1: 3: 3: 1) rows.
All sizes
16 (16: 16: 18: 18: 20: 20) rows of rib have now been completed.
Change to 4mm (US 6) needles.
3rd, 4th, and 5th sizes only
Now work in cable patt as folls:
Row 1 (RS): K to last 15 sts, P2, slip next 6 sts onto cable needle and leave at back of work, K4, slip the 2 P sts from cable needle back onto left needle and P these 2 sts, then K4 from cable needle, P2, K1.
Row 2 and every foll alt row: K3, (P4, K2) twice, P to end.
Row 3: K to last 15 sts, (P2, K4) twice, P2, K1.
Rows 5, 7 and 9: As row 3.
Row 10: As row 2.
These 10 rows form cable patt.
7th, 8th, 9th and 10th sizes only
Now work in cable patt as folls:
Row 1 (RS): (K2, K2tog) - (-: -: 0: 1: 1: 0) times, K to last 15 sts, P2, slip next 6 sts onto cable

needle and leave at back of work, K4, slip the 2 P sts from cable needle back onto left needle and P these 2 sts, then K4 from cable needle, P2, K1. - (-: -: 41: 44: 47: 51) sts.
Row 2 and every foll alt row: K3, (P4, K2) twice, P to end.
Row 3: (K2, K2tog) - (-: -: 1: 0: 0: 1) times, K to last 15 sts, (P2, K4) twice, P2, K1. - (-: -: 40: 44: 47: 50) sts.
Row 5: (K2, K2tog) - (-: -: 0: 1: 1: 0) times, K to last 15 sts, (P2, K4) twice, P2, K1. - (-: -: 40: 43: 46: 50) sts.
Row 7: As row 3.
Row 9: As row 5. - (-: -: 39: 42: 45: 49) sts.
Row 10: As row 2.
These 10 rows form cable patt.
Working all decreases as set, dec 1 st at beg of every foll - (-: -: -: -: 4th: 4th) row until - (-: -: -: -: 44: 47) sts rem.
Work - (-: -: 2: 6: 7: 7) rows, ending with a WS row.
Working all increases as set by back, inc 1 st at beg of next and every foll - (-: -: 6th: 8th: 6th: 8th) row until there are - (-: -: 44: 47: 50: 53) sts.
All sizes
Cont straight until left front matches back to beg of armhole shaping, ending with a WS row.
Shape armhole
Keeping cable patt correct, cast off 2 (2: 3: 3: 4: 4: 4) sts at beg of next row.
33 (36: 38: 41: 43: 46: 49) sts.
Work 1 row.
Dec 1 st at armhole edge of next 1 (1: 1: 3: 3: 3: 3) rows, then on foll 1 (2: 2: 1: 1: 2: 3) alt rows.
31 (33: 35: 37: 39: 41: 43) sts.
Cont straight until 12 (12: 12: 14: 14: 14: 14) rows less have been worked than on back to start of shoulder shaping, ending with a WS row.
Shape neck
Next row (RS): Patt 18 (20: 22: 24: 26: 27: 29) sts and turn, leaving rem 13 (13: 13: 13: 13: 14: 14) sts on a holder.
Work 1 row.
Dec 1 st at neck edge of next and every foll alt row until 14 (16: 18: 19: 21: 22: 24) sts rem.
Work 3 rows, ending with a WS row.
Shape shoulder
Cast off 5 (5: 6: 6: 7: 7: 8) sts at beg of next and foll alt row.
Work 1 row. Cast off rem 4 (6: 6: 7: 7: 8: 8) sts.

RIGHT FRONT
Cast on 35 (38: 41: 44: 47: 50: 53) sts using 3¼mm (US 3) needles and yarn A.
Row 1 (RS): K1, (P2, K4) twice, P2, *K2, P2, rep from * to last 0 (3: 2: 1: 0: 3: 2) sts, K0 (2: 2: 1: 0: 2: 2), P0 (1: 0: 0: 0: 1: 0).
Row 2: P0 (0: 0: 1: 0: 0: 0), K2 (1: 0: 2: 2: 1: 0), *P2, K2, rep from * to last 13 sts, (P4, K2) twice, K1.
These 2 rows form rib.
Work in rib for a further 14 (14: 14: 6: 8: 10: 12) rows, ending with a WS row.
7th, 8th, 9th and 10th sizes only
Dec 1 st at end of next and every foll 4th row until - (-: -: 41: 45: 48: 51) sts rem.
Work a further - (-: -: 1: 3: 3: 1) rows.
All sizes
16 (16: 16: 18: 18: 20: 20) rows of rib have now been completed.
Change to 4mm (US 6) needles.
3rd, 4th, and 5th sizes only
Now work in cable patt as folls:
Row 1 (RS): K1, P2, slip next 6 sts onto cable needle and leave at front of work, K4, slip the

2 P sts from cable needle back onto left needle and P these 2 sts, then K4 from cable needle, P2, K to end.

Row 2 and every foll alt row: P to last 15 sts, (K2, P4) twice, K3.

Row 3: K1, (P2, K4) twice, P2, K to end.

Rows 5, 7 and 9: As row 3.

Row 10: As row 2.

These 10 rows form cable patt.

7th, 8th, 9th and 10th sizes only

Now work in cable patt as folls:

Row 1 (RS): K1, P2, slip next 6 sts onto cable needle and leave at front of work, K4, slip the 2 P sts from cable needle back onto left needle and P these 2 sts, then K4 from cable needle, P2, K to last - (-: -: 0: 4: 4: 0) sts, (K2tog tbl, K2) - (-: -: 0: 1: 1: 0) times. - (: : 41: 44: 47: 51) sts.

Row 2 and every foll alt row: P to last 15 sts, (K2, P4) twice, K3.

Row 3: K1, (P2, K4) twice, P2, K to last - (-: -: 4: 0: 0: 4) sts, (K2tog tbl, K2) - (-: -: 1: 0: 0: 1) times.
- (-: -: 40: 44: 47: 50) sts.

Row 5: K1, (P2, K4) twice, P2, K to last - (-: -: 0: 4: 4: 0) sts, (K2tog tbl, K2) - (-: -: 0: 1: 1: 0) times. - (-: -: -: 40: 43: 46: 50) sts.

Row 7: As row 3.

Row 9: As row 5. - (-: -: -: 39: 42: 45: 49) sts.

Row 10: As row 2.

These 10 rows form cable patt.

All sizes

Complete to match left front, reversing shapings.

SLEEVES (both alike)

Cast on 42 (42: 42: 46: 46: 50: 50) sts using 3¼mm (US 3) needles and yarn B.

Row 1 (RS): P2, *K2, P2, rep from * to end.

Row 2: K2, *P2, K2, rep from * to end.

These 2 rows form rib.

Break off yarn B and join in yarn A.

Work in rib for a further 14 (14: 14: 16: 16: 18: 18) rows, ending with a WS row.

Change to 4mm (US 6) needles.

Beg with a K row, cont in st st as folls:
Work 2 rows.

Next row (RS): K2, M1, K to last 2 sts, M1, K2.

Working all increases as set by last row, inc 1 st at each end of every foll 10th (10th: 10th: 12th: 12th: 16th: 14th) row until there are 52 (54: 56: 58: 60: 62: 64) sts.

Cont straight until sleeve measures 21 (24: 27: 30: 33: 36: 39) cm, ending with a WS row.

Shape top

Cast off 2 (2: 3: 3: 4: 4: 4) sts at beg of next 2 rows. 48 (50: 50: 52: 52: 54: 56) sts.

Dec 1 st at each end of next 3 rows, then on foll 6 (7: 2: 2: 2: 2: 2) alt rows, then on every foll - (-: 4th: 4th: 4th: 4th: 4th) row until 30 (30: 38: 38: 36: 36: 38) sts rem.

6th, 7th, 8th, 9th and 10th sizes only

Work 1 row, ending with a WS row.

Dec 1 st at each end of next and every foll alt row until - (-: 30: 32: 32: 34: 34) sts rem.

All sizes

Dec 1 st at each end of next 5 rows, ending with a WS row.

Cast off rem 20 (20: 20: 22: 22: 24: 24) sts.

MAKING UP

PRESS as described on the information page. Join both shoulder seams using back stitch, or mattress st if preferred.

Collar

With RS facing, using 3¼mm (US 3) needles and yarn A, slip 13 (13: 13: 13: 13: 14: 14) sts of right front onto right needle, pick up and knit 12 (12: 12: 13: 13: 13: 13) sts up right side of neck, 22 (22: 22: 24: 24: 26: 26) sts from back, and 12 (12: 12: 13: 13: 13: 13) sts down left side of neck, then patt across 13 (13: 13: 13: 13: 14: 14) sts of left front. 72 (72: 72: 76: 76: 80: 80) sts.

Row 1 (WS): K3, *P2, K2, rep from * to last st, K1.

Row 2: K1, *P2, K2, rep from * to last 3 sts, P2, K1.

Rep these 2 rows until collar measures 5 (5: 5: 6: 6: 6: 6) cm, ending with a WS row.

Break off yarn A and join in yarn B.

Change to 3 mm (US 2/3) needles.

Beg with a K row, work in st st for 5 (5: 5: 6: 6: 6: 6) cm, ending with a WS row.

Cast off.

See information page for finishing instructions, setting in sleeves using the set-in method. Insert zip into front opening, positioning top of zip just below colour change of collar. Fold collar in half to inside and slip stitch in place.

Design number 22

Twinkle

YARN

Rowan Polar

		s/m	m/l		
A Winter White	645	1	1	x	100gm
B Silver Lining	646	1	1	x	100gm

NEEDLES

1 pair 8mm (no 0) (US 11) needles

TENSION

12 sts and 16 rows to 10 cm measured over stocking stitch using 8mm (US 11) needles.

FINISHED SIZE

Completed scarf is approx 11 (15) cm wide and 150 (200) cm long, 4 1/2 (6) in wide and 59 (79) in long.

SCARF

Cast on 17 (23) sts using 8mm (US 11) needles and yarn A.

Row 1 (RS): Using yarn A, knit.

Row 2: Using yarn A, P into front and back of first st, P to last 2 sts, P2tog.

Join in yarn B.

Row 3: Using yarn B, knit.

Row 4: Using yarn B, P into front and back of first st, P to last 2 sts, P2tog.

These 4 rows form patt.

Stranding yarn not in use loosely up side of work, cont in patt until scarf measures approx 150 (200) cm, ending after 2 rows using yarn A.

Cast off.

3rd, 4th & 5th sizes

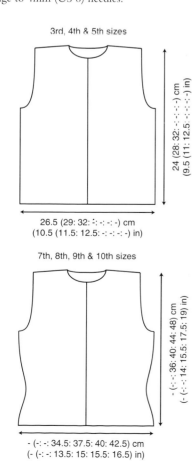

24 (28: 32: -: -: -: -) cm
(9.5 (11: 12.5: -: -: -: -) in)

26.5 (29: 32: -: -: -: -) cm
(10.5 (11.5: 12.5: -: -: -: -) in)

7th, 8th, 9th & 10th sizes

- (-: -: 36: 40: 44: 48) cm
(- (-: -: 14: 15.5: 17.5: 19) in)

- (-: -: 34.5: 37.5: 40: 42.5) cm
(- (-: -: 13.5: 15: 15.5: 16.5) in)

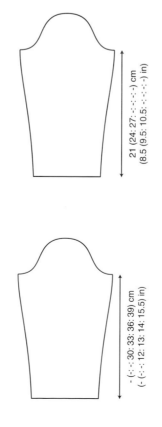

21 (24: 27: -: -: -: -) cm
(8.5 (9.5: 10.5: -: -: -: -) in)

- (-: -: 30: 33: 36: 39) cm
(- (-: -: 12: 13: 14: 15.5) in)

ZOE

YARN

		7th	8th	9th	10th	size
To fit age		6-7	8-9	9-10	11-12	years
To fit chest		66	71	76	81	cm
		26	28	30	32	in
Rowan Polar						
A Stormy	647	4	4	5	6	x 100gm
B Lettuce	642	1	1	1	1	x 100gm
C W White	645	1	1	2	2	x 100gm
B S Lining	646	1	2	2	2	x 100gm

NEEDLES

1 pair 7mm (no 2) (US 10½) needles
1 pair 8mm (no 0) (US 11) needles

TENSION

12 sts and 16 rows to 10 cm measured over
stocking stitch using 8mm (US 11) needles.

BACK

Cast on 55 (59: 63: 67) sts using 7mm (US 10½)
needles and yarn A.
Row 1 (RS): K2 (1: 3: 2), *P3, K3, rep from *
to last 5 (4: 6: 5) sts, P3, K2 (1: 3: 2).
Row 2: P2 (1: 3: 2), *K3, P3, rep from * to last
5 (4: 6: 5) sts, K3, P2 (1: 3: 2).
Rep these 2 rows twice more, end with a WS row.
Change to 8mm (US 11) needles.
Using a combination of the INTARSIA and
FAIRISLE techniques described on the info page,
starting and ending rows as indicated, omitting
part motifs at side edges for smallest size and beg
with a K row, work in patt from stag chart,
which is worked entirely in st st, until chart row
33 has been completed, ending with a RS row.
Break off all contrasts and cont in st st, beg with
a P row, using yarn A only.
Cont straight until back measures 29 (32: 35:
38) cm, ending with a WS row.
Shape armholes
Cast off 5 sts at beg of next 2 rows.
45 (49: 53: 57) sts.
Cont straight until armhole measures 20 (21: 22:
23) cm, ending with a WS row.
Shape shoulders and back neck
Cast off 5 (5: 6: 6) sts at beg of next 2 rows.
35 (39: 41: 45) sts.

Next row (RS): Cast off 5 (5: 6: 6) sts, K until
there are 9 (10: 9: 10) sts on right needle and
turn, leaving rem sts on a holder.
Work each side of neck separately.
Cast off 4 sts at beg of next row.
Cast off rem 5 (6: 5: 6) sts.
With RS facing, rejoin yarn to rem sts, cast off
centre 7 (9: 11: 13) sts, K to end.
Complete to match first side, reversing shapings.

FRONT

Work as given for back until 4 rows less have
been worked to beg of armhole shaping, ending
with a WS row.
Place snowflake chart
Join in yarn C and place snowflake motif as folls:
Next row (RS): K17 (19: 21: 23), starting with
chart row 1 and using the INTARSIA method
as described on the information page, work
across 21 sts from snowflake chart, K17 (19: 21:
23).
Next row: P17 (19: 21: 23), work row 2 from
chart, P17 (19: 21: 23).
These 2 rows set the sts − centre 21 sts worked
from chart with st st using yarn A at sides.
Work a further 2 rows, ending after chart row 4
and with a WS row.
Shape armholes
Keeping chart correct, cast off 5 sts at beg of
next 2 rows. 45 (49: 53: 57) sts.

Cont straight until chart row 21 has been
completed.
Break off yarn C and cont in st st using yarn A
only.
Cont straight until 8 rows less have been worked
than on back to start of shoulder shaping, ending
with a WS row.
Shape neck
Next row (RS): K19 (20: 21: 22) and turn,
leaving rem sts on a holder.
Work each side of neck separately.
Dec 1 st at neck edge of next 2 rows, then on
foll 2 alt rows. 15 (16: 17: 18) sts.
Work 1 row, ending with a WS row.
Shape shoulder
Cast off 5 (5: 6: 6) sts at beg of next and foll alt
row.
Work 1 row.
Cast off rem 5 (6: 5: 6) sts.
With RS facing, rejoin yarn to rem sts, cast off
centre 7 (9: 11: 13) sts, K to end.
Complete to match first side, reversing shapings.

SLEEVES (both alike)

Cast on 27 (29: 31: 33) sts using 7mm (US 10½)
needles and yarn A.
Row 1 (RS): K3 (1: 2: 3), *P3, K3, rep from *
to last 6 (4: 5: 6) sts, P3, K3 (1: 2: 3).
Row 2: P3 (1: 2: 3), *K3, P3, rep from * to last
6 (4: 5: 6) sts, K3, P3 (1: 2: 3).

Stag Chart

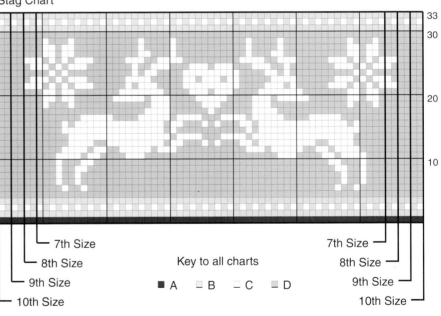

7th Size
8th Size
9th Size
10th Size

7th Size
8th Size
9th Size
10th Size

Key to all charts
■ A □ B ─ C ▨ D

Heart Chart

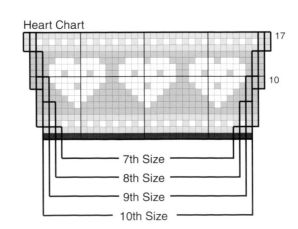

7th Size
8th Size
9th Size
10th Size

Snowflake Chart

Rep these 2 rows twice more, ending with a WS row.

Change to 8mm (US 11) needles.

Using a combination of the INTARSIA and FAIRISLE techniques described on the information page, starting and ending rows as indicated and beg with a K row, work in patt from heart chart, which is worked entirely in st st, until chart row 17 has been completed, ending with a RS row, **and at same time** inc 1 st at each end of chart row 3 and every foll 4th (4th: 6th: 6th) row. 35 (37: 37: 39) sts.

Break off all contrasts and cont in st st, beg with a P row, using yarn A only.

Inc 1 st at each end of 2nd (2nd: 4th: 4th) and every foll 4th (4th: 4th: 6th) row to 43 (51: 53: 49) sts, then on every foll alt (: : 4th) row until there are 49 (-: -: 55) sts.

Cont straight until sleeve measures 34 (38: 42: 46) cm, ending with a WS row.

Cast off.

MAKING UP

PRESS as described on the information page. Join right shoulder seam using back stitch, or mattress st if preferred.

Neckband

With RS facing, using 7mm (US 10½) needles and yarn A, pick up and knit 11 sts down left side of neck, 6 (9: 12: 12) sts from front, 11 sts up right side of neck, then 14 (17: 20: 20) sts from back. 42 (48: 54: 54) sts.

Row 1 (WS): ★P3, K3, rep from ★ to end.

Rep this row 5 times more.

Cast off in rib.

See information page for finishing instructions, setting in sleeves using the square set-in method.

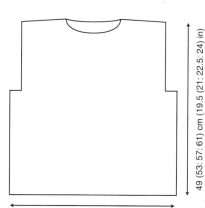

49 (53: 57: 61) cm (19.5 (21: 22.5: 24) in)

46 (49: 52.5: 56) cm (18 (19.5: 20.5: 22) in)

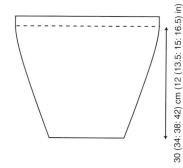

30 (34: 38: 42) cm (12 (13.5: 15: 16.5) in)

GRACE

YARN

Rowan Rowanspun DK

	6th	7th	8th	9th	10th size	
To fit age	4-5	6-7	8-9	9-10	11-12 years	
To fit chest	61	66	71	76	81	cm
	24	26	28	30	32	in

| **Plain cardigan** | 4 | 4 | 5 | 5 | 6 | x 50gm |

(photographed in Snowball 730)

Striped cardigan

| A Lavender 733 | 2 | 2 | 3 | 3 | 3 | x 50gm |
| B E de nil 735 | 2 | 2 | 3 | 3 | 3 | x 50gm |

NEEDLES

1 pair 3¼mm (no 10) (US 3) needles
1 pair 4mm (no 8) (US 6) needles

ZIP – open-ended zip to fit

TENSION

21 sts and 29 rows to 10 cm measured over stocking stitch using 4mm (US 6) needles.

Plain cardigan

Work as given for striped cardigan (below) but using one colour throughout.

Striped cardigan

BACK

Cast on 71 (77: 83: 89: 95) sts using 3¼mm (US 3) needles and yarn A.

Row 1 (RS): P1 (0: 1: 0: 1), K3 (1: 3: 1: 3), ★P3, K3, rep from ★ to last 1 (4: 1: 4: 1) sts, P1 (3: 1: 3: 1), K0 (1: 0: 1: 0).

Row 2: K1 (0: 1: 0: 1), P3 (1: 3: 1: 3), ★K3, P3, rep from ★ to last 1 (4: 1: 4: 1) sts, K1 (3: 1: 3: 1), P0 (1: 0: 1: 0).

These 2 rows form rib.

Work in rib for a further 4 (4: 6: 6: 6) rows, ending with a WS row.

Change to 4mm (US 6) needles.

Working next 4 (4: 2: 2: 2) rows using yarn A and then working in 20 row stripe sequence of 10 rows using yarn B and 10 rows using yarn A, cont in striped st st throughout, beg with a K row, as folls:

Dec 1 st at each end of 3rd (3rd: next: next: 3rd) and every foll 4th row until 61 (67: 71: 77: 83) sts rem.

Work 5 (7: 5: 7: 7) rows, ending with a WS row.

Inc 1 st at each end of next and every foll 6th row until there are 71 (77: 83: 89: 95) sts.

Work a further 7 (11: 7: 9: 13) rows, ending after 2 (8: 2: 6: 2) rows using yarn A (A: B: B: A) and with a WS row. (Back should measure 21 (23: 25: 26: 28) cm.)

Shape raglan armholes

Keeping stripes correct, cast off 5 sts at beg of next 2 rows. 61 (67: 73: 79: 85) sts.

Next row (RS): P2, K2tog, K to last 4 sts, K2tog tbl, P2.

Next row: K2, P2tog tbl, P to last 4 sts, P2tog, K2.

Working all raglan decreases as set by last 2 rows, dec 1 st at each end of next 5 rows, then on every foll alt row until 19 (21: 23: 25: 27) sts rem.

Work 1 row, ending after 10 (10: 8: 6: 6) rows using yarn B (A: B: A: B) and with a WS row.

Cast off.

LEFT FRONT

Cast on 36 (39: 42: 45: 48) sts using 3¼mm (US 3) needles and yarn A.

Row 1 (RS): P1 (0: 1: 0: 1), K3 (1: 3: 1: 3), ★P3, K3, rep from ★ to last 2 sts, P1, K1.

Row 2: K2, P3, ★K3, P3, rep from ★ to last 1 (4: 1: 4: 1) sts, K1 (3: 1: 3: 1), P0 (1: 0: 1: 0).

These 2 rows form rib.

Work in rib for a further 4 (4: 6: 6: 6) rows, ending with a WS row.

Change to 4mm (US 6) needles.

Working next 4 (4: 2: 2: 2) rows using yarn A and then working in 20 row stripe sequence of 10 rows using yarn B and 10 rows using yarn A, cont in striped st st, beg with a K row and with front opening edge st worked as a K st on every row, as folls:

Dec 1 st at beg of 3rd (3rd: next: next: 3rd) and every foll 4th row until 31 (34: 36: 39: 42) sts rem.

Work 5 (7: 5: 7: 7) rows, ending with a WS row.

Inc 1 st at beg of next and every foll 6th row until there are 36 (39: 42: 45: 48) sts.

Work a further 7 (11: 7: 9: 13) rows, ending with a WS row. (Left front should match back to beg of raglan armhole shaping.)

Shape raglan armhole
Keeping stripes correct, cast off 5 sts at beg of next row. 31 (34: 37: 40: 43) sts.
Work 1 row.
Working all raglan decreases as set by back raglan, dec 1 st at raglan edge of next 7 rows, then on every foll alt row until 16 (18: 19: 21: 22) sts rem, ending after 7 (5: 3: 9: 9) rows using yarn A (B: A: A: B) and with a RS row.

Shape neck
Cast off 6 (6: 7: 7: 8) sts at beg of next row.
10 (12: 12: 14: 14) sts.
Dec 1 st at neck edge of next 3 rows, then on foll 0 (1: 1: 2: 2) alt rows and at same time dec 1 st at raglan edge on next and every foll alt row. 5 sts.
Next row (WS): P3, K2.
Next row: P2, K3tog.
Next row: P1, K2.
Next row: P1, P2tog.
Next row: K2.
Next row: P2tog and fasten off.

RIGHT FRONT
Cast on 36 (39: 42: 45: 48) sts using 3¼mm (US 3) needles and yarn A.
Row 1 (RS): K1, P1, K3, ★P3, K3, rep from ★ to last 1 (4: 1: 4: 1) sts, P1 (3: 1: 3: 1), K0 (1: 0: 1: 0).
Row 2: K1 (0: 1: 0: 1), P3 (1: 3: 1: 3), ★K3, P3, rep from ★ to last 2 sts, K2.
These 2 rows form rib.
Work in rib for a further 4 (4: 6: 6: 6) rows, ending with a WS row.
Change to 4mm (US 6) needles.
Working next 4 (4: 2: 2: 2) rows using yarn A and then working in 20 row stripe sequence of 10 rows using yarn B and 10 rows using yarn A, cont in striped st st, beg with a K row and with front opening edge st worked as a K st on every row, as folls:
Dec 1 st at end of 3rd (3rd: next: next: 3rd) and every foll 4th row until 31 (34: 36: 39: 42) sts rem.
Complete to match Left Front, reversing shapings.

SLEEVES
Cast on 37 (43: 43: 49: 49) sts using 3¼mm (US 3) needles and yarn A.
Row 1 (RS): P2, ★K3, P3, rep from ★ to last 5 sts, K3, P2.
Row 2: K2, ★P3, K3, rep from ★ to last 5 sts, P3, K2.
These 2 rows form rib.
Work in rib for a further 4 (4: 6: 6: 6) rows, ending with a WS row.
Change to 4mm (US 6) needles.
Working next 4 (4: 2: 2: 2) rows using yarn A and then working in 20 row stripe sequence of 10 rows using yarn B and 10 rows using yarn A, cont in striped st st, beg with a K row, as folls:
Inc 1 st at each end of 5th (5th: 3rd: 3rd: 3rd) and every foll 6th (8th: 10th: 10th: 10th) row to 43 (49: 63: 53: 71) sts, then on every foll 8th (10th: –: 12th: –) row until there are 55 (59: –: 67: –) sts, taking inc sts into rib.
Work a further 11 rows, ending after 2 (8: 2: 6: 2) rows using yarn A (A: B: B: A) and with a WS row. (Sleeve should measure approx 28 (30: 39: 40: 42) cm.)

Shape raglan
Keeping stripes correct, cast off 5 sts at beg of next 2 rows. 45 (49: 53: 57: 61) sts.

Working all raglan decreases as set by back raglan, dec 1 st at each end of next and every foll 4th row to 41 (45: 47: 51: 55) sts, then on every foll alt row until 15 (15: 17: 17: 17) sts rem.
Work 1 row, ending with a WS row.

Left sleeve only
Dec 1 st at each end of next row.
13 (13: 15: 15: 15) sts.
Cast off 4 sts at beg of next row.
9 (9: 11: 11: 11) sts.
Dec 1 st at beg of next row, then cast off 4 (4: 5: 5: 5) sts at beg of foll row. 4 (4: 5: 5: 5) sts.

Right sleeve only
Cast off 5 sts at beg and dec 1 st at end of next row. 9 (9: 11: 11: 11) sts.
Work 1 row.
Cast off 4 (4: 5: 5: 5) sts at beg and dec 1 st at end of next row. 4 (4: 5: 5: 5) sts.
Work 1 row.

Both sleeves
Cast off rem 4 (4: 5: 5: 5) sts.

MAKING UP
PRESS as described on the information page.
Join raglan seams using back stitch, or mattress st if preferred.

Collar
Cast on 81 (87: 87: 93: 99) sts using 3¼mm (US 3) needles and yarn A.
Row 1 (RS): K3, ★P3, K3, rep from ★ to end.
Row 2: K1, P2, ★K3, P3; rep from ★ to last 6 sts, K3, P2, K1.
Rep last 2 rows until collar measures 8 cm, ending with a WS row.
Cast off in rib.
Sew cast-on edge of collar to neck edge, matching row ends at front opening edges.
See information page for finishing instructions, inserting zip behind front opening, positioning top of zip at neck edge.

SASHA

YARN

		s/m	m/l	
Rowan All Seasons Cotton				
A	Kiss	175	2	2	x 50gm
B	Valour	181	4	5	x 50gm

NEEDLES
1 pair 6½mm (no 3) (US 10½) needles

TENSION
18 sts and 21 rows to 10 cm measured over rib using 6½mm (US 10½) needles.

MEASUREMENTS
Finished scarf is approx 15 (22) cm wide by 193 (257) cm long, 6 (8½) in wide by 76 (101) in long.

SCARF
Cast on 27 (39) sts using 6½mm (US 10½) needles and yarn A.
Row 1 (RS): K3, ★P3, K3, rep from ★ to end.
Row 2: P3, ★K3, P3, rep from ★ to end.
These 2 rows form rib.
Work a further 34 rows using yarn A.
Join in yarn B.
Using yarn B, work 2 rows.
Using yarn A, work 6 rows.
Using yarn B, work 4 rows.
Using yarn A, work 4 rows.
Using yarn B, work 6 rows.
Using yarn A, work 2 rows.
Break off yarn A.
Using yarn B, cont straight until scarf measures 164 (228) cm, ending with a WS row.
Join in yarn A.
Using yarn A, work 2 rows.
Using yarn B, work 6 rows.
Using yarn A, work 4 rows.
Using yarn B, work 4 rows.
Using yarn A, work 6 rows.
Using yarn B, work 2 rows.
Break off yarn B.
Using yarn A, work a further 36 rows.
Cast off in rib.

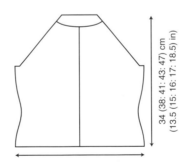

34 (36.5: 39.5: 42.5: 45) cm
(13.5 (14.5: 15.5: 16.5: 17.5) in)

34 (38: 41: 43: 47) cm
(13.5 (15: 16: 17: 18.5) in)

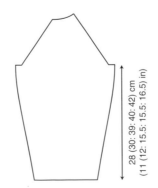

28 (30: 39: 40: 42) cm
(11 (12: 15.5: 15.5: 16.5) in)

ISLA

YARN

		s	m	l	
Rowan Kid Classic					
A Bewitch	830	1	1	2	x 50gm
Rowan Lurex Shimmer					
B Bedazzled	338	1	1	1	x 25gm

NEEDLES
1 pair 4mm (no 8) (US 6) needles
1 pair 5mm (no 6) (US 8) needles

TENSION
19 sts and 25 rows to 10 cm measured over stocking stitch using 5mm (US 8) needles.

MEASUREMENTS
Finished hat measures approx 37 (42: 48) cm, 14½ (16½: 19) in, around head.

HAT
Cast on 70 (82: 90) sts using 4mm (US 6) needles and yarn A.
Row 1 (RS): K2, *P2, K2, rep from * to end.
Row 2: P2, *K2, P2, rep from * to end.
Rep last 2 rows for 8 cm, inc (dec: inc) 1 st at end of last row and ending with a RS row. 71 (81: 91) sts.
Change to 5mm (US 8) needles.
Beg with a K row, work in st st throughout as folls:
Cont straight until hat measures 16 (18: 20) cm, ending with a P row.
Shape top
Row 1 (RS): *K8, K2tog, rep from * to last st, K1. 64 (73: 82) sts.
Work 3 rows.
Row 5: *K7, K2tog, rep from * to last st, K1. 57 (65: 73) sts.
Work 3 rows.
Row 9: *K6, K2tog, rep from * to last st, K1. 50 (57: 64) sts.
Work 3 rows.
Row 13: *K5, K2tog, rep from * to last st, K1. 43 (49: 55) sts.
Work 1 row.
Row 15: *K4, K2tog, rep from * to last st, K1.

JADE

YARN

		s/m	m/l	
Rowan Big Wool				
A White Hot	001	1	2	x 100gm
B Smoky	007	1	2	x 100gm

NEEDLES
1 pair 15mm (US 19) needles

TENSION
7½ sts and 10 rows to 10 cm measured over stocking stitch using 15mm (US 19) needles.

MEASUREMENTS
Finished scarf is approx 15 (19) cm wide by 160 (208) cm long, 6 (7½) in wide by 63 (82) in long, excluding fringe.

SCARF
Cast on 11 (14) sts using 15mm (US 19) needles and yarn A.
Row 1 (RS): Using yarn A, knit.
Row 2: Using yarn A, K2, P to last 2 sts, K2.
Rows 3 to 8: As rows 1 and 2, 3 times.
Join in yarn B.
Rows 9 to 16: As rows 1 and 2, 4 times **but using yarn B**.
Rep last 16 rows 9 (12) times more.
Cast off.
Fringe
Cut 18 (24) lengths of yarn A, each 32 cm long, and knot pairs of these threads through each st along cast-on edge, omitting edge sts. Trim ends even.
In same way, make fringe across cast-off edge using yarn B.

AMBER

YARN
Rowan All Seasons Cotton

	small	medium	large		
	1	2	2	x	50gm

(photographed in Organic 178)

NEEDLES
1 pair 4½mm (no 7) (US 7) needles

TENSION
20 sts and 24 rows to 10 cm measured over flattened rib using 4½mm (US 7) needles.

MEASUREMENTS
Finished hat measures approx 36 (40: 44) cm, 14 (15½: 17½) in, around head.

HAT
Cast on 72 (80: 88) sts using 4½mm (US 7) needles.
Row 1 (RS): *K2, P2, rep from * to end.
Row 2: As row 1.
These 2 rows form rib.
Cont in rib until hat measures 21 (23: 25) cm, ending with a WS row.
Shape top
Row 1 (RS): *K2tog, P2tog, rep from * to end. 36 (40: 44) sts.
Row 2: *K1, P1, rep from * to end.
Rep row 2, twice more.
Row 5 (RS): *K2tog, rep from * to end. 18 (20: 22) sts.
Row 6: *P2tog, rep from * to end.
Break yarn and thread through rem 9 (10: 11) sts.
Pull up tight and fasten off securely.
Join back seam, reversing seam for turn-back.

---

36 (41: 46) sts.
Work 1 row.
Row 17: *K3, K2tog, rep from * to last st, K1. 29 (33: 37) sts.
Work 1 row.
Row 19: *K2, K2tog, rep from * to last st, K1. 22 (25: 28) sts.

Row 20: *P2tog, rep from * to last 0 (1: 0) st, P0 (1: 0).
Break yarn and thread through rem 11 (13: 14) sts.
Pull up tight and fasten off securely.
Join back seam, reversing seam for turn-back.
Using yarn A and yarn B together, make 8 cm diameter pompom and attach to top of hat.

JASMINE

YARN

	7th	8th	9th	10th	size
To fit age	6-7	8-9	9-10	11-12	years
To fit chest	66	71	76	81	cm
	26	28	30	32	in

Rowan 4 ply Cotton

5	5	6	7	x	50gm

(photographed in Flirty 127)

NEEDLES

1 pair 2¼mm (no 13) (US 1) needles
1 pair 3mm (no 11) (US 2/3) needles
2¼mm (no 13) (US 1) circular needle

BUTTONS – 7 x 75315

TENSION

34 sts and 38 rows to 10 cm measured over pattern using 3mm (US 2/3) needles.

BACK

Cast on 429 (461: 493: 525) sts using 2¼mm (US 1) circular needle.
Row 1 (RS): K1, *K2, lift first of these 2 sts over 2nd st and off right needle, rep from * to end.
Row 2: P1, *P2tog, rep from * to end.**
108 (116: 124: 132) sts.
Change to 3mm (US 2/3) needles and work in lace patt as folls:
Row 1 (RS): K0 (2: 0: 0), P0 (1: 1: 0), K1 (2: 2: 1), *P1, yon, K2tog tbl, P1, K2, rep from * to last 5 (3: 1: 5) sts, (P1, yon, K2tog tbl) 1 (0: 0: 1) times, P1, K1 (2: 0: 1).
Row 2: P1 (2: 0: 1), *K1, P2, rep from * to last 2 (3: 1: 2) sts, K1, P1 (2: 0: 1).
Row 3: K0 (2: 0: 0), P0 (1: 1: 0), K1 (2: 2: 1), *P1, K2tog, yfrn, P1, K2, rep from * to last 5 (3: 1: 5) sts, (P1, K2tog, yfrn) 1 (0: 0: 1) times, P1, K1 (2: 0: 1).
Row 4: As row 2.
These 4 rows form lace patt.
Keeping lace patt correct throughout, cont as folls:
Work a further 2 rows.
Dec 1 st at each end of next and every foll 6th row to 102 (108: 114: 120) sts, then on every foll 4th row until 96 (102: 108: 114) sts rem.

Work 9 rows, ending with a WS row.
Inc 1 st at each end of next and every foll 4th row to 104 (112: 120: 126) sts, then on every foll 6th row until there are 108 (116: 124: 132) sts, taking inc sts into lace patt.
Cont straight until back measures 20 (23: 26: 29) cm, ending with a WS row.
Shape armholes
Keeping patt correct, cast off 4 (4: 5: 5) sts at beg of next 2 rows. 100 (108: 114: 122) sts.
Dec 1 st at each end of next 5 rows, then on foll 3 (4: 4: 5) alt rows, then on every foll 4th row until 80 (86: 92: 98) sts rem.
Cont straight until armhole measures 14 (15: 16: 17) cm, ending with a WS row.
Shape shoulders and back neck
Cast off 7 (8: 9: 9) sts at beg of next 2 rows. 66 (70: 74: 80) sts.
Next row (RS): Cast off 7 (8: 9: 9) sts, patt until there are 12 (12: 12: 14) sts on right needle and turn, leaving rem sts on a holder.
Work each side of neck separately.
Cast off 4 sts at beg of next row.
Cast off rem 8 (8: 8: 10) sts.
With RS facing, rejoin yarn to rem sts, cast off centre 28 (30: 32: 34) sts, patt to end.
Complete to match first side, reversing shapings.

LEFT FRONT
Cast on 217 (233: 249: 265) sts using 2¼mm (US 1) circular needle.
Work as given for back from ** to **.
55 (59: 63: 67) sts.
Change to 3mm (US 2/3) needles and work in lace patt as folls:
Row 1 (RS): K0 (2: 0: 0), P0 (1: 1: 0), K1 (2: 2: 1), *P1, yon, K2tog tbl, P1, K2, rep from * to end.
Row 2: P2, *K1, P2, rep from * to last 2 (3: 1: 2) sts, K1, P1 (2: 0: 1).
Row 3: K0 (2: 0: 0), P0 (1: 1: 0), K1 (2: 2: 1), *P1, K2tog, yfrn, P1, K2, rep from * to end.
Row 4: As row 2.
These 4 rows form lace patt.
Keeping lace patt correct throughout, cont as folls:
Work a further 2 rows.
Dec 1 st at beg of next and every foll 6th row to 52 (55: 58: 61) sts, then on every foll 4th row until 49 (52: 55: 58) sts rem.
Work 9 rows, ending with a WS row.
Inc 1 st at beg of next and every foll 4th row to 53 (57: 61: 64) sts, then on every foll 6th row until there are 55 (59: 63: 67) sts, taking inc sts into lace patt.

Cont straight until left front matches back to beg of armhole shaping, ending with a WS row.
Shape armhole
Keeping patt correct, cast off 4 (4: 5: 5) sts at beg of next row. 51 (55: 58: 62) sts.
Work 1 row.
Dec 1 st at armhole edge of next 5 rows, then on foll 3 (4: 4: 5) alt rows, then on every foll 4th row until 41 (44: 47: 50) sts rem.
Cont straight until 15 (15: 17: 17) rows less have been worked than on back to start of shoulder shaping, ending with a RS row.
Shape neck
Keeping patt correct, cast off 7 (8: 8: 9) sts at beg of next row, then 4 sts at beg of foll alt row.
30 (32: 35: 37) sts.
Dec 1 st at neck edge of next 7 rows, then on foll 1 (1: 2: 2) alt rows. 22 (24: 26: 28) sts.
Work 3 rows, ending with a WS row.
Shape shoulder
Cast off 7 (8: 9: 9) sts at beg of next and foll alt row.
Work 1 row.
Cast off rem 8 (8: 8: 10) sts.

RIGHT FRONT
Cast on 217 (233: 249: 265) sts using 2¼mm (US 1) circular needle.
Work as given for back from ** to **.
55 (59: 63: 67) sts.
Change to 3mm (US 2/3) needles and work in lace patt as folls:
Row 1 (RS): K2, *P1, yon, K2tog tbl, P1, K2, rep from * to last 5 (3: 1: 5) sts, (P1, yon, K2tog tbl) 1 (0: 0: 1) times, P1, K1 (2: 0: 1).
Row 2: P1 (2: 0: 1), *K1, P2, rep from * to end.
Row 3: K2, *P1, K2tog, yfrn, P1, K2, rep from * to last 5 (3: 1: 5) sts, (P1, K2tog, yfrn) 1 (0: 0: 1) times, P1, K1 (2: 0: 1).
Row 4: As row 2.
These 4 rows form lace patt.
Keeping lace patt correct throughout, cont as folls:
Work a further 2 rows.
Dec 1 st at end of next and every foll 6th row to 52 (55: 58: 61) sts, then on every foll 4th row until 49 (52: 55: 58) sts rem.
Complete to match left front, reversing shapings.

SLEEVES (both alike)
Cast on 213 (221: 229: 237) sts using 2¼mm (US 1) circular needle.
Work as given for back from ** to **.
54 (56: 58: 60) sts.

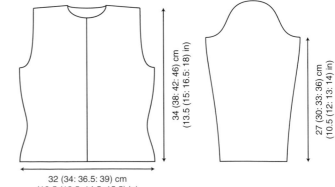

34 (38: 42: 46) cm
(13.5 (15: 16.5: 18) in)

32 (34: 36.5: 39) cm
(12.5 (13.5: 14.5: 15.5) in)

27 (30: 33: 36) cm
(10.5 (12: 13: 14) in)

Change to 3mm (US 2/3) needles and work in lace patt as folls:

Row 1 (RS): K1 (2: 0: 1), ★P1, yon, K2tog tbl, P1, K2, rep from ★ to last 5 (6: 4: 5) sts, P1, yon, K2tog tbl, P1, K1 (2: 0: 1).

Row 2: P1 (2: 0: 1), ★K1, P2, rep from ★ to last 2 (3: 1: 2) sts, K1, P1 (2: 0: 1).

Row 3: K1 (2: 0: 1), ★P1, K2tog, yfrn, P1, K2, rep from ★ to last 5 (6: 4: 5) sts, P1, K2tog, yfrn, P1, K1 (2: 0: 1).

Row 4: As row 2.

These 4 rows form lace patt.
Cont in lace patt, shaping sides by inc 1 st at each end of next and every foll 6th row until there are 82 (88: 94: 100) sts, taking inc sts into patt.
Cont straight until sleeve measures 27 (30: 33: 36) cm, ending with a WS row.

Shape top
Cast off 4 (4: 5: 5) sts at beg of next 2 rows.
74 (80: 84: 90) sts.

Dec 1 st at each end of next 7 rows, then on foll 3 alt rows, then on every foll 4th row until 48 (54: 56: 62) sts rem.
Work 1 row, ending with a WS row.
Dec 1 st at each end of next and foll 0 (1: 0: 1) alt row, then on foll 5 rows, ending with a WS row. 36 (40: 44: 48) sts.
Cast off 4 sts at beg of next 4 rows.
Cast off rem 20 (24: 28: 32) sts.

MAKING UP
PRESS as described on the information page.
Join shoulder seams using back stitch, or mattress st if preferred.

Button band
With RS facing and using 2¼mm (US 1) needles, starting at neck shaping, pick up and knit 96 (108: 120: 132) sts down left front opening edge, stopping 2 rows above cast-on edge.
Beg with a K row, work in rev st st for 4 rows.
Cast off knitwise (on WS).

Buttonhole band
With RS facing and using 2¼mm (US 1) needles, starting 2 rows above cast-on edge, pick up and knit 96 (108: 120: 132) sts up right front opening edge to neck shaping.
Row 1 (WS): K2, ★yfwd, K2tog, K13 (15: 17: 19), rep from ★ 5 times more, yfwd, K2tog, K2.
Beg with a P row, work in rev st st for 3 rows.
Cast off knitwise (on WS).

Neckband
With RS facing and using 2¼mm (US 1) needles, starting and ending halfway across top of bands, pick up and knit 26 (27: 29: 30) sts up right side of neck, 36 (38: 40: 42) sts from back, then 26 (27: 29: 30) sts down left side of neck. 88 (92: 98: 102) sts.
Beg with a K row, work in rev st st for 4 rows.
Cast off knitwise (on WS).
See information page for finishing instructions, setting in sleeves using the set-in method.

ALICE

YARN
Rowan Polar
2 x 100gm
(photographed in Blackforest 643)

For optional flower trim: Oddments of Rowan Kid Classic in main colour (Cherish 833) and contrast colour (Imp 829)

NEEDLES
1 pair 8mm (no 0) (US 11) needles
1 pair 4½mm (no 7) (US 7) needles for optional flower trim

TRIMMINGS
Piece of lining fabric 50 cm (19½ in) square (ref 95SC36)
60 cm of 3.5 cm wide petersham ribbon

TENSION
12 sts and 16 rows to 10 cm measured over stocking stitch using 8mm (US 11) needles.

FINISHED SIZE
Completed bag is approx 18 cm (7 in) wide, 17 cm (6½ in) tall and 7.5 cm (3 in) deep.

SIDES (make 2)
Cast on 5 sts using 8mm (US 11) needles.
Break yarn and set to one side for gusset.
Cast on 22 sts using 8mm (US 11) needles.
Beg with a K row, work in st st for 6 rows, ending with a WS row.

Shape for gussets
Next row (RS): Cast on and K 5 sts, slip next st (for gusset fold line), K20, slip next st (for gusset fold line), then K across gusset sts set to one side. 32 sts.
Next row: Purl.
Next row: K5, slip next st (for gusset fold line), K20, slip next st (for gusset fold line), K5.
Rep last 2 rows 14 times more, and then first of these 2 rows again, ending with a WS row.
Cast off.

HANDLES (make 2)
Cast on 9 sts using 8mm (US 11) needles.
Row 1 (RS): K2, slip next st (for fold line), K3, slip next st (for fold line), K2.
Row 2: Purl.
Rep these 2 rows 21 times more. Cast off.

FLOWER TRIM (optional)
Outer section
Cast on 79 sts using 4½mm (US 7) needles and main colour.
Row 1 (RS): Purl.
Row 2: K2, ★K1 and slip this st back onto left needle, lift next 8 sts on left needle over this st and off needle, (yfwd) twice, then K the same st again, K2, rep from ★ to end.★★
Row 3: K1, ★P2tog, (K1, K1 tbl) into double yfwd of previous row, P1, rep from ★ to last st, K1. 30 sts.
Row 4: Knit.
Row 5: (P2tog) 15 times.
Break yarn and thread through rem 15 sts. Pull up tight and fasten off securely. Join row ends.
Inner section
Work as given for outer section to ★★.
Break off main colour and join in contrast colour.

Work rows 3 and 4 as given for outer section.
Break yarn and thread through rem 30 sts. Pull up tight and fasten off securely. Join row ends.
Lay inner section onto outer section and sew together at centre.

MAKING UP
PRESS all pieces as described on the information page.
From lining fabric, cut 2 pieces same size as knitted side panels, adding seam allowance along all edges.
Join knitted side panels along cast-on edges (base) and row-end edges (sides). Fold bag so that base/side seams meet and row-end edges of base match cast-on edges of side gussets, and sew seams. Fold 3 cm to inside around upper edge and slip stitch in place.
Cut petersham ribbon into two equal lengths and wrap knitted handles around each strip. Slip stitch row-end edges of handles together to enclose petersham, positioning seam centrally along strip. Positioning handles approx 6 cm apart, sew ends of handles in position inside upper edge of sides of bag.
Make up lining in same way as main knitted sections and slip lining inside bag. Turn under raw edge around top of bag and slip stitch lining in place.
Attach optional flower trim as in photograph.

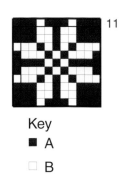

HANNAH

YARN
Rowan Polar

			s	m	l	
A	Red Hot	641	1	1	1	x 100gm
B	Winter White	645	1	1	1	x 100gm

NEEDLES
1 pair 7½mm (no 2) (US 10½) needles
1 pair 8mm (no 0) (US 11) needles

TENSION
12 sts and 16 rows to 10 cm measured over stocking stitch using 8mm (US 11) needles.

MEASUREMENTS
Finished hat measures approx 41 (46: 51) cm, 16 (18: 20) in, around head.

HAT
Cast on 49 (55: 61) sts using 7½mm (US 10½) needles and yarn A.
Row 1 (RS): K1, *P1, K1, rep from * to end.
Row 2: P1, *K1, P1, rep from * to end.
Rep last 2 rows once more.
Change to 8mm (US 11) needles.
Beg with a K row, work in st st throughout as folls:
Work 2 rows.
Join in yarn B.
Using yarn B, work 2 rows.
Break off yarn B.
Work 2 rows in yarn A.
Place chart
Join in yarn B and place motif as folls:
Next row (RS): K19 (22: 25), starting with chart row 1 and using the INTARSIA method as described on the information page, work across 11 sts from chart, K to end.
Next row: P19 (22: 25), work across 11 sts from chart, P to end.
These 2 rows set the sts – centre 11 sts worked from chart with st st using yarn A at sides.
Cont straight until chart row 11 has been completed.
Break off yarn B and cont in st st using yarn A only.
Work a further 1 (3: 5) rows, ending with a WS row.

Shape top
Row 1 (RS): *K4, K2tog, rep from * to last st, K1. 41 (46: 51) sts.
Work 1 row.
Row 3: *K3, K2tog, rep from * to last st, K1. 33 (37: 41) sts.
Work 1 row.
Row 5: *K2, K2tog, rep from * to last st, K1. 25 (28: 31) sts.
Row 6: P1, *P2tog, P1, rep from * to end. 17 (19: 21) sts.
Row 7: *K2tog, rep from * to last st, K1.
Break yarn and thread through rem 9 (10: 11) sts.
Pull up tight and fasten off securely.
Join back seam. Using yarn B, make 8 cm diameter pompom and attach to top of hat.

DYLAN

YARN
Rowan 4 ply Soft

			small	medium	large	
A	Sooty	372	1	1	1	x 50gm
B	Nippy	376	1	1	1	x 50gm

NEEDLES
1 pair 3mm (no 11) (US needles
1 pair 3¼mm (no 10) (US 3) needles

TENSION
28 sts and 36 rows to 10 cm measured over stocking stitch using 3¼mm (US 3) needles.

MEASUREMENTS
Finished hat measures approx 38 (41: 44) cm, 15 (16: 17½) in, around head.

HAT
Cast on 107 (115: 123) sts using 3mm (US 2/3) needles and yarn A.
Beg with a K row, work in st st throughout as folls:
Using yarn A, work 2 rows.
Join in yarn B.

Using yarn B, work 2 rows.
These 4 rows form stripe patt.
Cont in stripe patt for a further 4 rows.
Change to 3¼mm (US 3) needles.
Cont straight until hat measures 24 (25: 26) cm, ending with a WS row.
Shape top
Keeping stripes correct, cont as folls:
Large size only
Row 1 (RS): K1, K2tog, *K27, K3tog tbl, rep from * twice more, K27, K2tog tbl, K1. 115 sts.
Work 1 row.
Medium and large size only
Next row (RS): K1, K2tog, *K25, K3tog tbl, rep from * twice more, K25, K2tog tbl, K1. 107 sts.
Work 1 row.
All sizes
Next row (RS): K1, K2tog, *K23, K3tog tbl, rep from * twice more, K23, K2tog tbl, K1. 99 sts.
Work 1 row.
Next row: K1, K2tog, *K21, K3tog tbl, rep from * twice more, K21, K2tog tbl, K1. 91 sts.
Work 1 row.
Next row: K1, K2tog, *K19, K3tog tbl, rep from * twice more, K19, K2tog tbl, K1. 83 sts.
Work 1 row.
Next row: K1, K2tog, *K17, K3tog tbl, rep from * twice more, K17, K2tog tbl, K1. 75 sts.
Work 1 row.
Next row: K1, K2tog, *K15, K3tog tbl, rep from * twice more, K15, K2tog tbl, K1. 67 sts.
Work 1 row.
Next row: K1, K2tog, *K13, K3tog tbl, rep from * twice more, K13, K2tog tbl, K1. 59 sts.
Work 1 row.
Next row: K1, K2tog, *K11, K3tog tbl, rep from * twice more, K11, K2tog tbl, K1. 51 sts.
Next row: P1, P2tog tbl, *P9, P3tog tbl, rep from * twice more, P9, P2tog, P1. 43 sts.
Next row: K1, K2tog, *K7, K3tog tbl, rep from * twice more, K7, K2tog tbl, K1. 35 sts.
Next row: P1, P2tog tbl, *P5, P3tog tbl, rep from * twice more, P5, P2tog, P1. 27 sts.
Next row: K1, K2tog, *K3, K3tog tbl, rep from * twice more, K3, K2tog tbl, K1. 19 sts.
Next row: P1, P2tog tbl, *P1, P3tog tbl, rep from * twice more, P1, P2tog, P1. 11 sts.
Break yarn and thread through rem 11 sts. Pull up tight and fasten off securely.
Join back seam. Fold 8 cm to inside around cast-on edge and slip stitch in place.

11

Key
■ A
□ B

CALLUM

YARN

	6th	7th	8th	9th	10th size
To fit age	4-5	6-7	8-9	9-10	11-12 years
To fit chest	61	66	71	76	81 cm
	24	26	28	30	32 in

Rowan Polar 4 4 5 5 6 x100gm
(photographed in Stony 640)

NEEDLES
1 pair 7mm (no 2) (US 10½) needles
1 pair 8mm (no 0) (US 11) needles

ZIP
Open-ended zip to fit

TENSION
12 sts and 16 rows to 10 cm measured over stocking stitch using 8mm (US 11) needles.

BACK
Cast on 43 (47: 51: 55: 59) sts using 7mm (US 10½) needles.
Work in garter st for 8 rows, ending with a WS row.

Change to 8mm (US 11) needles.
Beg with a K row, cont in st st as folls:
Cont straight until back measures 28 (29: 30: 31: 33) cm, ending with a WS row.
Shape raglan armholes
Cast off 5 sts at beg of next 2 rows.
33 (37: 41: 45: 49) sts.
9th and 10th sizes only
Next row (RS): P2, K2tog, K to last 4 sts, K2tog tbl, P2.
Next row: K2, P2tog tbl, P to last 4 sts, P2tog, K2.
All sizes
Next row (RS): P2, K2tog, K to last 4 sts, K2tog tbl, P2.
Next row: K2, P to last 2 sts, K2.
Working all raglan decreases as set by last 2 rows, dec 1 st at each end of next and every foll alt row until 11 (13: 15: 15: 17) sts rem.
Work 1 row, ending with a WS row.
Cast off rem 11 (13: 15: 15: 17) sts.

LEFT FRONT
Cast on 22 (24: 26: 28: 30) sts using 7mm (US 10½) needles.
Work in garter st for 8 rows, ending with a WS row.
Change to 8mm (US 11) needles.
Next row (RS): Knit.
Next row: K1, P to end.
These 2 rows set the sts – front opening edge st worked as a K st on every row with all other sts in st st.
Keeping sts correct as set, cont as folls:
Cont straight until left front matches back to beg of raglan armhole shaping, ending with a WS row.
Shape raglan armhole
Cast off 5 sts at beg of next row.
17 (19: 21: 23: 25) sts.
Work 1 row.
Working all raglan decreases as set by back, dec 1 st at raglan edge of next 1 (1: 1: 3: 3) rows, then on foll alt row. 15 (17: 19: 19: 21) sts.
Work 1 row, ending with a WS row.
Shape front slope
Dec 1 st at each end of next and every foll alt row until 5 sts rem.
Work 1 row, ending with a WS row.
Next row (RS): P2, K3tog. 3 sts.
Next row: P1, K2.
Next row (RS): P3tog.
Next row: K1 and fasten off.

RIGHT FRONT
Cast on 22 (24: 26: 28: 30) sts using 7mm (US 10½) needles.
Work in garter st for 8 rows, ending with a WS row.
Change to 8mm (US 11) needles.
Next row (RS): Knit.
Next row: P to last st, K1.
These 2 rows set the sts.
Complete to match left front, reversing shapings.

SLEEVES
Cast on 29 (29: 31: 31: 33) sts using 7mm (US 10½) needles.
Work in garter st for 8 rows, ending with a WS row.
Change to 8mm (US 11) needles.
Beg with a K row, cont in st st, shaping sides by inc 1 st at each end of 3rd and every foll 8th (8th: 8th: 8th: 10th) row to 33 (33: 41: 41: 37) sts, then on every foll 6th (6th: 6th: 6th: 8th) row until there are 39 (41: 43: 45: 47) sts.
Cont straight until sleeve measures 27 (31: 35: 39: 43) cm, ending with a WS row.
Shape raglan
Cast off 5 sts at beg of next 2 rows.
29 (31: 33: 35: 37) sts.
Working all raglan decreases as set by back and front raglans, dec 1 st at each end of next and every foll alt row until 11 sts rem.
Work 1 row, ending with a WS row.
Left sleeve only
Dec 1 st at each end of next row. 9 sts.
Cast off 2 sts at beg of next row. 7 sts.
Dec 1 st at beg of next row, then cast off 3 sts at beg of foll row. 3 sts.
Right sleeve only
Cast off 3 sts at beg and dec 1 st at end of next row. 7 sts.
Work 1 row.
Rep last 2 rows once more. 3 sts.
Both sleeves
Cast off rem 3 sts.

MAKING UP
PRESS as described on the information page.
Join raglan seams using back stitch, or mattress st if preferred.
Collar
Cast on 2 sts using 7mm (US 10½) needles.
(This point matches to beg of left front slope shaping.)
Work in garter st, shaping neck edge by inc 1 st at beg of next and every foll alt row until there are 17 sts, then on foll 4th row. 18 sts.
Cont straight until shaped edge of collar, **unstretched**, fits up left front slope, across top of sleeve and across to centre back neck.
Cast off.
Work second collar section in same way, reversing shaping.
Join cast-off edges of collar to form back neck seam, then sew shaped edge of collar to neck edge.
See information page for finishing instructions.
Insert zip into front opening.

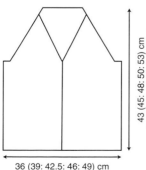

36 (39: 42.5: 46: 49) cm
(14 (15.5: 16.5: 18: 19.5) in)

43 (45: 48: 50: 53) cm
(17 (17.5: 19: 19.5: 21) in)

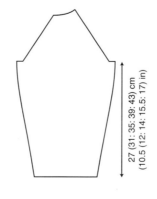

27 (31: 35: 39: 43) cm
(10.5 (12: 14: 15.5: 17) in)

LOTUS

YARN

	1st	2nd	3rd	4th	5th	size
To fit age	months					
	0-6	6-12	1-2	2-3	3-4	years
To fit chest	41	46	51	56	58	cm
	16	18	20	22	23	in
Rowan All Seasons Cotton						
A Kiss	175 1	1	1	1	1	x 50gm
Rowan Wool Cotton						
B Rich	911 2	2	3	3	3	x 50gm

	6th	7th	8th	9th	10th	size
To fit age	4-5	6-7	8-9	9-10	11-12	years
To fit chest	61	66	71	76	81	cm
	24	26	28	30	32	in
Rowan All Seasons Cotton						
A Kiss	175 2	2	2	2	2	x 50gm
Rowan Wool Cotton						
B Rich	911 4	4	5	5	6	x 50gm

NEEDLES

1 pair 4mm (no 8) (US 6) needles

TENSION

22 sts and 30 rows to 10 cm measured over stocking stitch using yarn B and 4mm (US 6) needles.

BACK

Cast on 33 (39: 45: 45: 51: 45: 51: 51: 57: 63) sts using 4mm (US 6) needles and yarn A.
Row 1 (RS): K3, *P3, K3, rep from * to end.
Row 2: P3, *K3, P3, rep from * to end.
These 2 rows form rib.
Work in rib for a further 10 (10: 10: 12: 12: 14: 14: 16: 16: 16) rows, ending with a WS row.
Break off yarn A and join in yarn B.
Next row (inc) (RS): K3 (3: 4: 3: 6: 3: 3: 6: 1), M1, *K2 (3: 4: 3: 4: 3: 4: 3: 3: 4), M1, rep from * to last 4 (3: 5: 3: 4: 6: 4: 3: 6: 2) sts, K to end.
47 (51: 55: 59: 63: 57: 63: 67: 73: 79) sts.
Beg with a P row, cont in st st as folls:
6th, 7th, 8th, 9th and 10th sizes only
Work 1 row, ending with a WS row.
Next row (inc) (RS): K2, M1, K to last 2 sts, M1, K2.
Working all increases as set by last row, inc 1 st at

each end of every foll - (-: -: -: -: 6th: 8th: 8th: 8th: 10th) row until there are - (-: -: -: -: -: 67: 73: 79: 85: 91) sts.

All sizes
Cont straight until back measures 10 (12: 13: 14: 16: 18: 20: 23: 25: 27) cm, ending with a WS row.
Shape raglan armholes
Cast off 3 (3: 3: 4: 4: 4: 5: 5: 5: 5) sts at beg of next 2 rows. 41 (45: 49: 51: 55: 59: 63: 69: 75: 81) sts.
1st, 2nd, 3rd, 4th, 5th, 6th and 7th sizes only
Next row (dec) (RS): P2, K2tog, K to last 4 sts, K2tog tbl, P2.
Next row: K2, P to last 2 sts, K2.
Next row: P2, K to last 2 sts, P2.
Next row: K2, P to last 2 sts, K2.
Rep last 4 rows 3 (2: 2: 2: 2: 1: 1: -: -: -) times more. 33 (39: 43: 45: 49: 55: 59: -: -: -) sts.
9th and 10th sizes only
Next row (dec) (RS): P2, K2tog, K to last 4 sts, K2tog tbl, P2.
Next row: K2, P2tog tbl, P to last 4 sts, P2tog, K2.
Rep last 2 rows - (-: -: -: -: -: -: -: 0: 2) times more. - (-: -: -: -: -: -: -: 71: 69) sts.
All sizes
Next row (dec) (RS): P2, K2tog, K to last 4 sts, K2tog tbl, P2.
Next row: K2, P to last 2 sts, K2.
Rep last 2 rows 6 (9: 10: 11: 12: 15: 16: 21: 21: 20) times more.
Cast off rem 19 (19: 21: 21: 23: 23: 25: 25: 27: 27) sts.

FRONT

Work as given for back until 31 (31: 33: 33: 35: 37: 39: 39: 41: 41) sts rem in raglan shaping.
Work 1 row, ending with a WS row.
Shape neck
Next row (RS): P2, K2tog, K4 (4: 4: 4: 4: 6: 6: 6: 6: 6) and turn, leaving rem sts on a holder.
Work each side of neck separately.
Dec 1 st at neck edge of next 2 rows, then on foll 0 (0: 0: 0: 0: 1: 1: 1: 1: 1) alt row **and at same time** dec 1 st at raglan edge of 2nd and foll - (-: -: -: -: alt: alt: alt: alt: alt) row. 4 sts.

Next row (WS): P2, K2.
Next row: (P2tog) twice. 2 sts.
Next row: K2.
Next row: P2tog and fasten off.
With RS facing, rejoin yarn to rem sts, cast off centre 15 (15: 17: 17: 19: 17: 19: 19: 21: 21) sts, K to last 4 sts, K2tog tbl, P2.
Complete to match first side, reversing shapings.

SLEEVES

Cast on 27 (27: 27: 33: 33: 33: 33: 39: 39: 39) sts using 4mm (US 6) needles and yarn A.
Work in rib as given for back for 10 (10: 10: 12: 12: 14: 14: 16: 16: 16) rows, ending with a WS row.
Break off yarn A and join in yarn B.
Next row (inc) (RS): K3 (1: 3: 4: 1: 2: 3: 2: 2: 1), M1, *K7 (5: 3: 8: 6: 4: 3: 7: 5: 4), M1, rep from * to last 3 (1: 3: 5: 2: 3: 3: 2: 2: 2) sts, K to end.
31 (33: 35: 37: 39: 41: 43: 45: 47: 49) sts.
Beg with a P row, cont in st st as folls:
Work 1 row, ending with a WS row.
Next row (inc) (RS): K2, M1, K to last 2 sts, M1, K2.
Working all increases 2 sts in from ends of row as set by last row, inc 1 st at each end of every foll 3rd (4th: 5th: 6th: 7th: 8th: 9th: 10th: 11th: 12th) row until there are 47 (49: 51: 53: 55: 57: 59: 61: 63: 65) sts.
Cont straight until sleeve measures 14 (17: 20: 23: 26: 29: 32: 35: 38: 41) cm, ending with a WS row.
Shape raglan
Cast off 3 (3: 3: 4: 4: 4: 5: 5: 5: 5) sts at beg of next 2 rows.
41 (43: 45: 45: 47: 49: 49: 51: 53: 55) sts.
1st, 2nd and 3rd sizes only
Next row (dec) (RS): P2, K2tog, K to last 4 sts, K2tog tbl, P2.
Next row: K2, P2tog tbl, P to last 4 sts, P2tog, K2. 37 (39: 41: -: -: -: -: -: -: -) sts.
7th, 8th, 9th and 10th sizes only
Next row (dec) (RS): P2, K2tog, K to last 4 sts, K2tog tbl, P2.

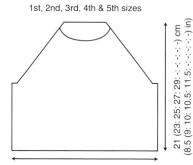

1st, 2nd, 3rd, 4th & 5th sizes

21.5 (23: 25: 27: 28.5: -: -: -: -: -) cm
(8.5 (9: 10: 10.5: 11: -: -: -: -: -) in)

21 (23: 25: 27: 29: -: -: -: -: -) cm
(8.5 (9: 10: 10.5: 11.5: -: -: -: -: -) in)

6th, 7th, 8th, 9th, & 10th sizes

- (-: -: -: -: 30.5: 33: 36: 38.5: 41.5) cm
(- (-: -: -: -: 12: 13: 14: 15: 16.5) in)

- (-: -: -: -: 32: 35: 38: 41: 44) cm
(- (-: -: -: -: 12.5: 14: 15: 16: 17.5) in)

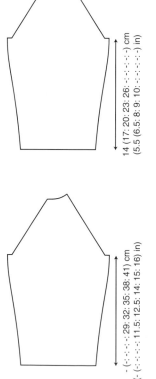

14 (17: 20: 23: 26: -: -: -: -: -) cm
(5.5 (6.5: 8: 9: 10: -: -: -: -: -) in)

- (-: -: -: -: 29: 32: 35: 38: 41) cm
(- (-: -: -: -: 11.5: 12.5: 14: 15: 16) in)

Next row: K2, P to last 2 sts, K2.
Next row: P2, K to last 2 sts, P2.
Next row: K2, P to last 2 sts, K2.
Rep last 4 rows once more.
- (-: -: -: -: -: 45: 47: 49: 51) sts.
All sizes
Next row (dec) (RS): P2, K2tog, K to last
4 sts, K2tog tbl, P2.
Next row: K2, P to last 2 sts, K2.
Working all decreases as set by last 2 rows, dec 1 st
at each end of next and every foll alt row until
15 (15: 15: 15: 15: 15: 17: 17: 17: 17) sts rem.
Work 1 row, ending with a WS row.
Left sleeve only
Dec 1 st at each end of next row, then cast off
2 sts at beg of foll row.

11 (11: 11: 11: 11: 11: 13: 13: 13: 13) sts.
Dec 1 st at beg of next row, then cast off 3 (3: 3:
3: 3: 3: 4: 4: 4: 4) sts at beg of foll row.
7 (7: 7: 7: 7: 7: 8: 8: 8: 8) sts.
Rep last 2 rows once more. 3 sts.
Right sleeve only
Cast off 3 sts at beg and dec 1 st at end of next
row. 11 (11: 11: 11: 11: 11: 13: 13: 13: 13) sts.
Work 1 row.
Cast off 3 (3: 3: 3: 3: 3: 4: 4: 4: 4) sts at beg and
dec 1 st at end of next row.
7 (7: 7: 7: 7: 7: 8: 8: 8: 8) sts.
Work 1 row.
Rep last 2 rows once more. 3 sts.
Both sleeves
Cast off rem 3 sts.

MAKING UP
PRESS as described on the information page.
Join both front and right back raglan seams
using back stitch, or mattress st if preferred.
Neckband
With RS facing, using 4mm (US 6) needles and
yarn A, pick up and knit 9 (9: 9: 10: 10: 10: 11:
11: 12: 12) sts from left sleeve, 25 (25: 25: 27: 27:
27: 28: 28: 30: 30) sts from front, 9 (9: 9: 10: 10:
10: 11: 11: 12: 12) sts from right sleeve, then
14 (14: 14: 16: 16: 16: 19: 19: 21: 21) sts from
back. 57 (57: 57: 63: 63: 63: 69: 69: 75: 75) sts.
Work in rib as given for back for 5 (5: 5: 6: 6: 6:
7: 7: 7: 7) cm.
Cast off **loosely** in rib.
See information page for finishing instructions.

DESIGN NUMBER 35

FELIX

YARN

Rowan Handknit DK Cotton

	1st	2nd	3rd	4th	5th	size
To fit age						
		months		years		
	0-6	6-12	1-2	2-3	3-4	
To fit chest						
	41	46	51	56	58	cm
	16	18	20	22	23	in
A Tope 253 or Muddy 302						
	1	1	2	2	2	x 50gm
B Linen 205 or Chime 204						
	3	3	4	5	6	x 50gm

	6th	7th	8th	9th	10th	size
To fit age						
	4-5	6-7	8-9	9-10	11-12	years
To fit chest						
	61	66	71	76	81	cm
	24	26	28	30	32	in
A Tope 253 or Muddy 302						
	3	3	3	4	4	x 50gm
B Linen 205 or Chime 204						
	7	8	9	11	12	x 50gm

NEEDLES
1 pair 3¼mm (no 10) (US 3) needles
1 pair 4mm (no 8) (US 6) needles

TENSION
20 sts and 28 rows to 10 cm measured over
stocking stitch using 4mm (US 6) needles.

BACK
Cast on 47 (57: 62: 72: 77: 87: 97: 102: 112: 117) sts
using 3¼mm (US 3) needles and yarn A.
Row 1 (RS): P2, *K3, P2, rep from * to end.
Row 2: K2, *P3, K2, rep from * to end.
These 2 rows form rib.
Work in rib for a further 14 (16: 18: 22: 24: 26:
26: 28: 28: 28) rows, - (dec: inc: dec: inc: -: dec:
inc: dec: inc) - (1: 1: 1: 1: -: 1: 1: 1: 1) st at
- (both: one: one: both: -: both: one: one: both)
end(s) of last row and ending with a WS row.
47 (55: 63: 71: 79: 87: 95: 103: 111: 119) sts.
Break off yarn A and join in yarn B.
Change to 4mm (US 6) needles.
Beg with a K row, cont in st st as folls:
Cont straight until back measures 11 (13: 15: 18:
21: 24: 27: 30: 33: 36) cm, ending with a WS row.
Shape armholes
Cast off 5 sts at beg of next 2 rows.
37 (45: 53: 61: 69: 77: 85: 93: 101: 109) sts.
Cont straight until armhole measures 12 (14: 16:
17: 18: 19: 20: 21: 22: 23) cm, end with a WS row.
Shape shoulders and back neck
Cast off 2 (4: 5: 6: 7: 8: 9: 10: 11: 12) sts at beg of
next 2 rows.
33 (37: 43: 49: 55: 61: 67: 73: 79: 85) sts.
Next row (RS): Cast off 2 (4: 5: 6: 7: 8: 9: 10:
11: 12) sts, K until there are 7 (7: 8: 9: 11: 12: 13:
15: 16: 17) sts on right needle and turn, leaving
rem sts on a holder.
Work each side of neck separately.
Cast off 4 sts at beg of next row.
Cast off rem 3 (3: 4: 5: 7: 8: 9: 11: 12: 13) sts.
With RS facing, rejoin yarn to rem sts, cast off
centre 15 (15: 17: 19: 19: 21: 23: 23: 25: 27) sts,
K to end.
Complete to match first side, reversing shapings.

FRONT
Work as given for back until 10 rows less have
been worked than on back to start of shoulder
shaping, ending with a WS row.
Shape neck
Next row (RS): K12 (16: 19: 22: 26: 29: 32: 36:
39: 42) and turn, leaving rem sts on a holder.
Work each side of neck separately.
Dec 1 st at neck edge of next 4 rows, then on
foll alt row. 7 (11: 14: 17: 21: 24: 27: 31: 34: 37) sts.
Work 3 rows, ending with a WS row.
Shape shoulder
Cast off 2 (4: 5: 6: 7: 8: 9: 10: 11: 12) sts at beg of
next and foll alt row.

Work 1 row.
Cast off rem 3 (3: 4: 5: 7: 8: 9: 11: 12: 13) sts.
With RS facing, rejoin yarn to rem sts, cast off
centre 13 (13: 15: 17: 17: 19: 21: 21: 23: 25) sts, K
to end.
Complete to match first side, reversing shapings.

SLEEVES (both alike)
Cast on 37 (37: 42: 42: 47: 47: 47: 47: 52: 52) sts
using 3¼mm (US 3) needles and yarn A.
Work in rib as given for back for 16 (18: 20: 24:
26: 28: 28: 30: 30: 30) rows, ending with a WS
row, **and at same time** inc 1 st at each end of
11th (11th: 11th: 13th: 13th: 15th: 15th: 15th:
15th: 15th) and every foll 4th (alt: alt: alt: 4th:
4th: 4th: 4th: 4th) row, taking inc sts into rib.
41 (45: 52: 54: 55: 55: 55: 55: 60: 60) sts.
Break off yarn A and join in yarn B.
Change to 4mm (US 6) needles.
Beg with a K row, cont in st st as folls:
Inc 1 st at each end of 3rd (next: next: next: 3rd:
3rd: 3rd: next: next: next) and every foll 4th row
to 49 (57: 64: 68: 73: 77: 81: 81: 72: 72) sts, then
on every foll - (-: -: -: -: -: -: 6th: 6th: 6th) row
until there are - (-: -: -: -: -: -: 85: 88: 92) sts.

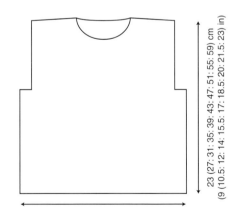

23.5 (27.5: 31.5: 35.5: 39.5: 43.5: 47.5: 51.5: 55.5: 59.5) cm
(9.5 (11: 12.5: 14: 15.5: 17: 18.5: 20.5: 22: 23.5) in)

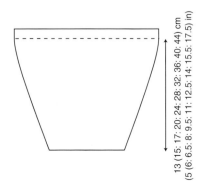

Cont straight until sleeve measures 15.5 (17.5: 19.5: 22.5: 26.5: 30.5: 34.5: 38.5: 42.5: 46.5) cm, ending with a WS row. Cast off.

MAKING UP
PRESS as described on the information page. Join right shoulder seam using back stitch, or mattress st if preferred.

Neckband
With RS facing, using 3¼mm (US 3) needles and yarn B, pick up and knit 14 sts down left side of neck, 12 (12: 15: 17: 17: 19: 22: 22: 22: 25) sts from front, 14 sts up right side of neck, then 22 (22: 24: 27: 27: 30: 32: 32: 32: 34) sts from back. 62 (62: 67: 72: 72: 77: 82: 82: 82: 87) sts.
Beg with a WS row, work in rib as given for back for 6 rows.
Beg with a P row, work in st st for 5 rows.
Cast off **loosely** knitwise.
See information page for finishing instructions, setting in sleeves using the square set-in method.

MYA

YARN

	1st	2nd	3rd	4th	5th	size
	months		years			
To fit age	0-6	6-12	1-2	2-3	3-4	
To fit chest	41	46	51	56	58	cm
	16	18	20	22	23	in
Rowan 4 ply Soft						
A Buzz 375	2	3	4	4	5	x 50gm
B Sooty 372	1	1	1	1	1	x 50gm
C Nippy 376	1	1	1	1	1	x 50gm

NEEDLES
2¾mm (no 12) (US 2) circular needle
3mm (no 11) (US 2/3) circular needle
1 pair 3¼mm (no 10) (US 3) needles

BUTTONS – 2 x 75320

TENSION
28 sts and 36 rows to 10 cm measured over stocking stitch using 3¼mm (US 3) needles.

BACK and FRONTS
(worked in one piece to armholes)
Cast on 189 (207: 231: 249: 273) sts using 2¾mm (US 2) circular needle and yarn C.
**Now work in stripe patt as folls:
Row 1 (RS): Using yarn C, knit, now push all sts back to opposite end of needle, ready to start next row at beg of previous row.
Row 2 (RS): Using yarn B, knit.
Row 3 (WS): Using yarn C, purl, now push all sts back to opposite end of needle, ready to start next row at beg of previous row.
Row 4 (WS): Using yarn B, purl.
These 4 rows form stripe patt.

Work in stripe patt for a further 4 rows.
Change to 3mm (US 2/3) circular needle.
Work a further 6 rows in stripe patt.
Break off yarn B and yarn C.
Join in yarn A and cont using yarn A only.
Change to 3¼mm (US 3) needles.**
Next row (RS): Knit.
Next row (WS): (P1, K1) twice, P to last 4 sts, (K1, P1) twice.
Next row: (P1, K1) twice, K to last 4 sts, (K1, P1) twice.
These 2 rows set the sts – 4 sts in moss st at each end with st st between.
Keeping sts correct as set, cont straight until work measures 8.5 (11.5: 14.5: 17.5: 20.5) cm, ending with a WS row.

Shape front slopes
Place markers at both ends of last row.
Cast off 8 (9: 10: 11: 12) sts at beg of next 2 rows, then 5 (5: 6: 6: 7) sts at beg of foll 4 rows.
153 (169: 187: 203: 221) sts.

Divide for armholes
Next row (RS): Cast off 5 (5: 6: 6: 7) sts, K until there are 36 (41: 45: 50: 54) sts on right needle after cast-off and slip these sts onto a holder for right front, cast off 8 sts, K until there are 55 (61: 69: 75: 83) sts on right needle after cast-off and slip these sts onto another holder for back, cast off 8 sts, K to end.

Shape left front
Work on this last set of sts only for left front.
Cast off 5 (5: 6: 6: 7) sts at beg of next row.
36 (41: 45: 50: 54) sts.
Dec 1 st at front slope edge of next 2 rows.
Work 1 row.
Rep last 3 rows 7 (9: 7: 11: 9) times more.
20 (21: 29: 26: 34) sts.
Dec 1 st at front slope edge of next and foll 4 (3: 8: 3: 8) alt rows. 15 (17: 20: 22: 25) sts.
Work a further 3 rows, ending with a WS row.
(Armhole should measure 10.5 (11.5: 12.5: 13.5: 14.5) cm.)

Shape shoulder
Cast off 5 (6: 7: 7: 8) sts at beg of next and foll alt row.
Work 1 row. Cast off rem 5 (5: 6: 8: 9) sts.

Shape back
With WS facing, rejoin yarn to 55 (61: 69: 75: 83) sts left on holder for back.
Beg with a P row, work straight in st st until back matches left front to start of shoulder shaping, ending with a WS row.

Shape shoulders and back neck
Cast off 5 (6: 7: 7: 8) sts at beg of next 2 rows.
45 (49: 55: 61: 67) sts.
Next row (RS): Cast off 5 (6: 7: 7: 8) sts, K until there are 9 (9: 10: 12: 13) sts on right needle and turn, leaving rem sts on a holder.
Work each side of neck separately.
Cast off 4 sts at beg of next row.
Cast off rem 5 (5: 6: 8: 9) sts.
With RS facing, rejoin yarn to rem sts, cast off centre 17 (19: 21: 23: 25) sts, K to end.
Complete to match first side, reversing shapings.

Shape right front
With WS facing, rejoin yarn to 36 (41: 45: 50: 54) sts left on holder for right front.
Beg with a P row, cont in st st and complete to match left front, reversing shapings.

SLEEVES (both alike)
Cast on 37 (39: 41: 43: 45) sts using 2¾mm (US 2) circular needle and yarn C.
Work as given for back and fronts from ** to **.
Beg with a K row, cont in st st, shaping sides by inc 1 st at each end of next and every foll 4th row to 41 (51: 61: 73: 83) sts, then on every foll alt (alt: alt: alt: -) row until there are 59 (65: 71: 77: -) sts.
Cont straight until sleeve measures 14 (17: 21: 25: 29) cm, ending with a WS row.
Cast off.

MAKING UP
PRESS as described on the information page.
Join shoulder seams using back stitch, or mattress st if preferred.

Front band
With RS facing, using 2¾mm (US 2) circular needle and yarn A, starting and ending at markers, pick up and knit 61 (66: 74: 77: 85) sts up right side of neck, 25 (27: 29: 31: 33) sts from back, then 61 (66: 74: 77: 85) sts down left side of neck. 147 (159: 177: 185: 203) sts.
Row 1 (WS): K1, *P1, K1, rep from * to end.
Rep this row 4 times more.
Cast off in moss st.
Join sleeve seams, leaving 1.5 cm open at upper edge. Fold first 7 rows to inside around lower edge of body and sleeves and slip stitch in place.
See information page for finishing instructions, setting in sleeves using the square set-in method.
Make buttonloops at row ends of front band and attach buttons to side seams to correspond (one button on outside, and other button on inside).

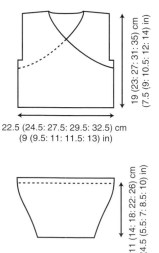

19 (23: 27: 31: 35) cm
(7.5 (9: 10.5: 12: 14) in)

22.5 (24.5: 27.5: 29.5: 32.5) cm
(9 (9.5: 11: 11.5: 13) in)

11 (14: 18: 22: 26) cm
(4.5 (5.5: 7: 8.5: 10) in)

LUCY

YARN

Rowan Big Wool

	4th	5th	6th	size	
To fit age	2-3	3-4	4-5	years	
To fit chest	56	58	61	cm	
	22	23	24	in	
	3	4	4	x	100gm

	7th	8th	9th	10th	size	
To fit age	6-7	8-9	9-10	11-12	years	
To fit chest	66	71	76	81	cm	
	26	28	30	32	in	
	5	6	6	7	x100gm	

(photographed in Sherbet Lime 002)

NEEDLES

1 pair 15mm (US 19) needles
15mm (US 19) circular needle

TENSION

7½ sts and 10 rows to 10 cm measured over stocking stitch using 15mm (US 19) needles.

BACK and FRONT

(after hem sections, worked in one piece to armholes)

Back hem section
Cast on 27 (29: 31: 33: 35: 37: 39) sts using 15mm (US 19) needles.
Work in garter st for 9 rows, ending with **wrong** side row.
Break yarn and leave sts on a holder.

Front hem section

Cast on 27 (29: 31: 33: 35: 37: 39) sts using 15mm (US 19) needles.
Work in garter st for 9 rows, ending with **wrong** side row.

Join sections
Change to 15mm (US 19) circular needle and work in rounds as folls:
Next round (RS): K across 27 (29: 31: 33: 35: 37: 39) sts of front hem section, then K across 27 (29: 31: 33: 35: 37: 39) sts of back hem section. 54 (58: 62: 66: 70: 74: 78) sts.
Place marker on needle to denote beg and end of rounds and left side seam.
Working in **rounds** of st st (by working every round as a K round), cont straight until work measures 19 (21: 23: 25: 29: 31: 35) cm from cast-on edge, ending 3 sts before side seam marker.

Divide for armholes
Next row (RS): Cast off 6 sts, K until there are 21 (23: 25: 27: 29: 31: 33) sts on right needle after cast off and slip these sts onto a holder for front, cast off next 6 sts, K to end and turn.
Work on this set of 21 (23: 25: 27: 29: 31: 33) sts only for back.
Change to 15mm (US 19) needles.
Cont in **rows** of st st, beg with a P row, until armhole measures 16 (18: 20: 22: 22: 24: 24) cm, ending with a WS row.

Shape shoulder
Next row (RS): K6 (6: 7: 7: 8: 8: 9) and slip these sts onto a holder for right shoulder, cast off next 9 (11: 11: 13: 13: 15: 15) sts for back neck, K to end and slip these last 6 (6: 7: 7: 8: 8: 9) sts onto another holder for left shoulder.
With WS facing, rejoin yarn to sts left on front holder and cont in **rows** of st st, beg with a P row, until 6 (6: 6: 6: 8: 8: 8) rows less have been worked than on back to shoulder cast-off, ending with a WS row.

Shape neck
Next row (RS): K8 (8: 9: 9: 11: 11: 12) and turn, leaving rem sts on a holder.
Work each side of neck separately.
Dec 1 st at neck edge of next 2 rows, then on foll 0 (0: 0: 0: 1: 1: 1) alt row. 6 (6: 7: 7: 8: 8: 9) sts.
Work 3 rows, ending with a WS row.

Join left shoulder seam
With WS together and working with RS of front towards you, join left shoulder seam by cast off 6 (6: 7: 7: 8: 8: 9) sts of front together with back left shoulder sts left on holder.
With RS facing, rejoin yarn to rem sts, cast off centre 5 (7: 7: 9: 7: 9: 9) sts, K to end.
Complete to match first side, reversing shapings.

SLEEVES

Cast on 15 (17: 19: 21: 21: 23: 23) sts using 15mm (US 19) needles.

Work in garter st for 9 rows, inc 1 st at each end of 4th (6th: 8th: 8th: 8th: 8th: 8th) and foll 4th (-: -: -: -: -: -) row and ending with **wrong** side row. 19 (19: 21: 23: 23: 25: 25) sts.
Beg with a K row, cont in st st, shaping sides by inc 1 st at each end of 3rd (next: 5th: 3rd: 5th: 5th: 5th) and every foll 4th (6th: 6th: 6th: 6th: 6th: 6th) row until there are 23 (25: 27: 31: 31: 35: 35) sts.
Cont straight until sleeve measures 23 (29: 33: 37: 41: 45: 49) cm, ending with a WS row.
Cast off.

MAKING UP

PRESS as described on the information page.
Neckband
With RS facing and using 15mm (US 19) circular needle, starting and ending at left shoulder seam, pick up and knit 6 (6: 6: 6: 8: 8: 8) sts down left side of neck, 5 (7: 7: 9: 7: 9: 9) sts from front, 6 (6: 6: 6: 8: 8: 8) sts up right side of neck, then 9 (11: 11: 13: 13: 15: 15) sts from back. 26 (30: 30: 34: 36: 40: 40) sts.
Round 1 (RS): Purl.
Round 2 (RS): Knit.
Rep last 2 rounds twice more.
Cast off purlwise.
See information page for finishing instructions, setting in sleeves using the square set-in method.

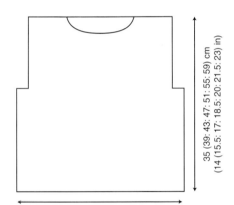

35 (39: 43: 47: 51: 55: 59) cm
(14 (15.5: 17: 18.5: 20: 21.5: 23) in)

36 (38.5: 41.5: 44: 46.5: 49.5: 52) cm
(14 (15: 16.5: 17.5: 18.5: 19.5: 20.5) in)

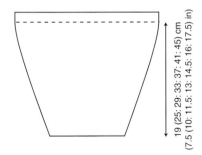

19 (25: 29: 33: 37: 41: 45) cm
(7.5 (10: 11.5: 13: 14.5: 16: 17.5) in)

INFORMATION PAGE

TENSION

Obtaining the correct tension is perhaps the single factor which can make the difference between a successful garment and a disastrous one. It controls both the shape and size of an article, so any variation, however slight, can distort the finished look of the garment. No-one wants to spend hours and hours making a "skinny rib" when they really want a "sloppy Joe".

Within each pattern there may be different tensions given, for instance, if either **Intarsia** or **Fairisle** techniques **and stocking stitch** are used in the same design. We strongly advise that you knit a square in pattern and or stocking stitch (depending on the pattern instruction) of perhaps 5 - 10 more stitches and 5 - 10 more rows than those given in the tension note. Place the finished square on a flat surface and measure the central area. If you have too many stitches to 10cm try again using thicker needles, if you have too few stitches to 10cm try again using finer needles. Once you have achieved the correct tension your garment will be knitted to the measurements given in the pattern.

SIZE NOTE

The instructions are given for the smallest size. Where they vary, work the figures in brackets for the larger sizes. One set of figures refers to all sizes. For ease in reading charts it may be helpful to have the chart enlarged at a printers and then to outline the size you intend to knit on the chart.

CHART NOTE

Many of the patterns in the book are worked from charts. Each square on a chart represents a stitch and each line of squares a row of knitting. When working from the charts, read odd rows (K) from right to left and even rows (P) from left to right, unless otherwise stated. Each colour used is given a different symbol or letter and these are shown in the **materials** section, or in the **key** alongside the chart of each pattern.

KNITTING WITH COLOUR

There are two main methods of working colour into a knitted fabric: **Intarsia** and **Fairisle** techniques. The first method produces a single thickness of fabric and is usually used where a colour is only required in a particular area of a row and does not form a repeating pattern across the row, as in the fairisle technique.

Intarsia: The simplest way to do this is to cut short lengths of yarn for each motif or block

of colour used in a row. Then joining in the various colours at the appropriate point on the row, link one colour to the next by twisting them around each other where they meet on the wrong side to avoid gaps. All ends can then either be darned along the colour join lines, as each motif is completed or then can be "knitted-in" to the fabric of the knitting as each colour is worked into the pattern. This is done in much the same way as "weaving-in" yarns when working the Fairisle technique and does save time darning-in ends. It is essential that the tension is noted for **Intarsia** as this may vary from the stocking stitch if both are used in the same pattern.

Fairisle type knitting: When two or three colours are worked repeatedly across a row, strand the yarn **not** in use loosely behind the stitches being worked. If you are working with more than two colours, treat the "floating" yarns as if they were one yarn and always spread the stitches to their correct width to keep them elastic. It is advisable not to carry the stranded or "floating " yarns over more than three stitches at a time, but to weave them under and over the colour you are working. The "floating" yarns are therefore caught at the back of the work.

ALL ribs should be knitted to a firm tension, for some knitters it may be necessary to use a smaller needle. In order to prevent sagging in cuffs and welts we suggest you use a "knitting-in" elastic.

PRESSING

After working for hours knitting a garment, it seems a great pity that many garments are spoiled because so little care is taken in the pressing and finishing. After darning in all the ends, block each piece of knitting. Press each piece, except ribs, gently, using a warm iron over a damp cloth. Take special care to press the edges as this will make the sewing up both easier and neater.

FINISHING INSTRUCTIONS

When stitching the pieces together match the colour patterns very carefully. Use a back stitch for all main knitting seams and an edge to edge stitch for all ribs unless otherwise stated.

Join left shoulder seam using back stitch and neckband seam (where appropriate) using an edge to edge stitch.

Sleeves

Set-in sleeves: Set in sleeve easing sleeve head into armhole using back stitch.

Square set-in sleeve: Set sleeve head into armhole, the straight sides at top of sleeve to form a neat right-angle to cast off sts at armhole on back and front, using back stitch.

Shallow set-in sleeves: Join cast-off sts at beg of armhole shaping to cast-off sts at start of sleeve-head shaping. Sew sleeve-head into armhole, easing in shapings.

Join side and sleeve seams using back stitch.

Slip stitch pocket edgings and linings into place.

Sew on buttons to correspond with button-holes.

After sewing up, press seams and hems. Ribbed welts and neckbands and any areas of garter stitch should not be pressed.

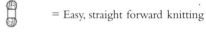

= Easy, straight forward knitting

= Suitable for the average knitter

ABBREVIATIONS

K	knit
P	purl
st(s)	stitch(es)
inc	increas(e)(ing)
dec	decreas(e)(ing)
st st	stocking stitch (1 row K, 1 row P)
garter st	garter stitch (K every row)
beg	begin(ning)
foll	following
rem	remain(ing)
rev	revers(e)(ing)
rep	repeat
alt	alternate
cont	continue
patt	pattern
tog	together
mm	millimetres
cm	centimetres
in(s)	inch(es)
RS	right side
WS	wrong side
sl1	slip one stitch
psso	pass slipped stitch over
tbl	through back of loop
M1	make one stitch by picking up horizontal loop before next stitch and knitting into back of it
yfwd	yarn forward
yrn	yarn round needle
yon	yarn over needle
yfrn	yarn forward and round needle

ROWAN OVERSEAS DISTRIBUTORS

AUSTRALIA
Australian Country Spinners
314 Albert Street
Brunswick
Victoria 3056
Tel: (03) 9380 3801

BELGIUM
Pavan
Koningin Astridlaan 78
B9000 Gent
Tel: (32) 9 221 8594

CANADA
Diamond Yarn
9697 St Laurent
Montreal
Quebec
H3L 2N1
Tel: (514) 388 6188
www.diamondyarns.com

Diamond Yarn (Toronto)
155 Martin Ross
Unit 3
Toronto
Ontario
M3J 2L9
Tel: (416) 736 6111
www.diamondyarns.com

DENMARK
Individual stockists -
please contact Rowan for
details

FRANCE
Elle Tricot
8 Rue du Coq
67000 Strasbourg
Tel: (33) 3 88 23 03 13
www.elletricote.com

GERMANY
Wolle & Design
Wolfshovener Strasse 76
52428 Julich-Stetternich
Tel : (49) 2461 54735.
www.wolleundesign.de

HOLLAND
de Afstap
Oude Leliestraat 12
1015 AW Amsterdam
Tel : (31) 20 6231445

HONG KONG
East Unity Co Ltd
Unit B2
7/F, Block B
Kailey Industrial Centre
12 Fung Yip Street
Chai Wan
Tel : (852) 2869 7110.

ICELAND
Storkurinn
Kjorgardi
Laugavegi 59
Reykjavik
Tel: (354) 551 82 58

JAPAN
DiaKeito Co Ltd
2-3-11 Senba-Higashi
Minoh City
Osaka
Tel : (81) 727 27 6604
www.rowanintl-jp.com

NEW ZEALAND
Individual stockists -
please contact Rowan for
details

NORWAY
Hera
Tennisun 3D
0777 OSLO
Tel: (47) 22 49 54 65

SWEDEN
Wincent
Norrtulsgaten 65
11345 Stockholm
Tel: (46) 8 33 70 60

U.S.A.
Rowan USA
5 Northern Boulevard
Amherst
New Hampshire 03031
Tel: (1 603) 886 5041/5043